D1715347

"A must-read for parents, grandparents, teachers, youth pastors, or anyone with a heart for teens. . . . A story of redemption and restoration. I challenge you to take in all that the author has to offer in order to help the teens in your life navigate the uncertainty of their world."

—**David Runnels**, former Youth Director at Northern Hills United Methodist Church

"The candor and willingness in which Dee Dee shares her story is truly inspirational. Speaking from experience as a school counselor, so many students get entrenched in unhealthy relationships . . . . This book is a wonderful resource with information for people dealing with all aspects of this critical issue. I look forward to using it as resource as I work with youth and others in my life, and I look forward to recommending the book to others."

—**Alicia Edwards**, Counselor, Byron P. Steele High School, Schertz-Cibolo-Universal City ISD

"Dee Dee's ordeal serves as a guide for what parents can do and watch for in their own children. This honest narrative gives insight into why it's hard to leave. I never knew girls would say yes to boys or go out with them to avoid hurting their feelings. In talking with my daughter, it's more common than I realized. The book touches on a lot of influences in kids' lives and calls out for parents to be mindful."

—**John Allen**, Principal Software Engineer—IT, Dell Computers

"With a heart and passion for helping teenagers and families, Dee Dee recounts her personal experience with teen dating abuse; depicting the slow transitions, sharing red flags, providing statistics that show how vast abusive relationships are, and lets the reader know they are not alone. She then shares ways of helping someone in an abusive relationship. *It Doesn't Start with a Punch* provides beneficial information from beginning to end."

—**Celeste Inman**, M.Ed., LPC-S, RPT-S

"The value of *It Doesn't Start with a Punch* is endless. The author's story of how a smart, caring person becomes involved with an abuser is consistent with experiences I've witnessed throughout life and as a teacher. Many of the signs discussed are common in abusive relationships. Her ability to take her story, link it to known psychological information and statistics, and then find a path to healing is exemplary. As a christian I loved her connections between everyday struggles and direct quotes from the Bible. This is a must-read!"

—**Ingeri Milam**, Christian, mother, and high school teacher

"Honest. Raw. Smart. Dee Dee tells a compelling story of a young woman's heartbreaking search for love and acceptance. Rejoice with Dee Dee as she shares the secret that allowed her to break free of the bonds that had held her captive to bad choices and destructive behavior."

—**John Mitchell**, Lt. Colonel (retired), US Air Force

It Doesn't Start with a Punch

It Doesn't Start with a Punch

My Journey through an Abusive Teen Dating Relationship

Dee Dee Said

Building Strong
Foundations

Scripture quotations marked ESV are from The ESV® Bible (The Holy Bible, English Standard Version®), copyright © 2001 by Crossway, a publishing ministry of Good News Publishers. Used by permission. All rights reserved. All other Scripture quotations are taken from the Holy Bible, New International Version®, NIV®. Copyright © 1973, 1978, 1984, 2011 by Biblica, Inc.™ Used by permission of Zondervan. All rights reserved worldwide. www.zondervan.com "NIV" and "New International Version" are trademarks registered in the United States Patent and Trademark Office by Biblica, Inc.™

This memoir is a recollection of actual events in the author's life. The events, places, conversations, and chronology are portrayed truthfully, to the best of Dee Dee Said's memory. While all characters portrayed in this book are real people, names and identifying characteristics of some individuals have been changed to respect their privacy. The author does not harbor any negative feelings toward her abuser nor wish him harm in any way. She is sharing her story only in the hope of helping adults and teens understand how abuse starts and grows so that others—victims as well as perpetrators—can be helped.

The content of this book is for informational purposes only. The information and suggestions are not intended to serve as a substitute for consultation with a qualified healthcare provider. For matters regarding your mental and physical health or that of someone you know, please seek the advice of a licensed counselor, physician, or other healthcare provider. If you or someone you know is in a life-threatening or emergency situation, seek professional assistance immediately. Neither the author, publisher, nor editors are engaged in rendering professional advice to the reader, nor shall they be liable or responsible for any loss or damage allegedly arising from any information or suggestions in this book.

Printed in the United States of America
San Antonio, TX

Published by: Building Strong Foundations, LLC
Info@BSFtoday.com

Developmental editing: Elizabeth Zach
Proofreading: Beth Bazar & Christina Roth

Copyediting: Courtney Oppel & Karen Stocz Oemler
Design: Sarah Lahay (www.cestbeaudesigns.com)

ISBN: 979-8-9866957-0-9

Library of Congress Control Number: 2022914613

Publisher's Cataloging-in-Publication Data

Names: Said, Dee Dee, 1970- author. Title: It doesn't start with a punch : my journey through an abusive teen dating relationship / by Dee Dee Said. Description: San Antonio, TX : Building Strong Foundations, LLC, [2022] | Includes bibliographical references. Identifiers: ISBN: 979-8-9866957-0-9 (paperback) | 979-8-9866957-1-6 (ebook) | LCCN: 2022914613 Subjects: LCSH: Victims of dating violence--Services for--Religious apects--Christianity. | Abused teenagers--Services for--Religious aspects--Christianity. | Sexually abused teenagers-- Services for--Religious aspects--Christianity. | Dating violence--Prevention. | Teenage girls--Abuse of--Prevention. | Teenage girls--Crimes against--Prevention. | Dating (Social customs) | Teenagers--Social life and customs. | Abusive men--Psychological aspects. | Self-actualization (Psychology) | LCGFT: Autobiographies. | BISAC: FAMILY & RELATIONSHIPS / Abuse / Domestic Partner Abuse. | FAMILY & RELATIONSHIPS / Life Stages / Adolescence. | RELIGION / Christian Living / Personal Growth. | BIOGRAPHY & AUTOBIOGRAPHY / Personal Memoirs. Classification: LCC: HQ801.83 .S25 2022 | DDC: 362.88/083--dc23

Contents

The light shines in the darkness,
and the darkness has not overcome it.

(John 1:5)

Thank you, God, for calling my name and healing me.

Thank you, Jesus, for showing us how to live while in this world.

Thank you, Holy Spirit, for whispering the way to go.

Introduction
A Whisper from God

Hello, Friend,

During Sunday school class several years ago, God whispered a special message to me. The message not only healed my heart but is meant to be shared so it can help others.

The message came to me through a video by Bill Hybels, a pastor, author, and instructor of church leaders, titled *The Power of a Whisper: Hearing God, Having the Guts to Respond.* The video alternates between snippets of different people's stories, gradually building each story as several people share what God told each of them. In one of the stories, a mother starts talking about the day her sixteen-year-old daughter drove by herself to her first day of work. Shortly after the daughter leaves for work, the home phone rings. As the mother goes to answer it, she hears the words, "**This doesn't change who you are. I still love you.**"

When the mother answers the phone, the person on the other end informs her that her daughter has been in a car accident and is in critical condition. As the mom's story unfolds, the viewers learn the daughter passes away. As the mother strives to move forward through the days and weeks after this terrible, heart-wrenching accident, she keeps hearing the words God spoke to her. They give her a feeling of inner peace and strength.

As soon as I heard this woman share her story, I knew that God was delivering the very same message to me. Even though the trauma I endured earlier in my life is very different from the loss this mother experienced, God's message immediately had a profound impact on me.

First, I heard and accepted the message that **God loved me**. Second, over the next several weeks His loving message began to release me from the shame and guilt I'd buried deep inside myself and carried for more than twenty long years.

You see, as a teenager, I dated a boy. You might be surprised to learn that this teen emotionally and physically abused me for three years before I found the strength and courage to leave him. While I was in that relationship, I believed *I* was the cause of all the anger and abuse he unleashed on me.

When the relationship ended, I essentially slammed the door behind me so I could move forward with my life. But I also did something else that I should not have done: I shut the door on the pain, hurt, anger, isolation, fear, shame, and guilt I'd experienced in that relationship. Because I didn't deal with those feelings, I didn't heal.

I ended up carrying those feelings inside me for over two decades, allowing them to continue to hurt me and pull me away from others and God. As a result, and because of the choices I'd made and the beliefs I'd developed while in that relationship, I came to think I was a bad person. Hearing God's words through that video helped me realize for the first time that **being in an abusive relationship was something that happened to me and did not change who I was on the inside**. Certainly, it affected me, but it didn't make me a bad person.

If you are in or have been the victim of an abusive relationship, please know that many people love and care about you. God loves you. What has happened to you does not change the valuable, worthy person you are.

As I accepted God's message, I also began to sense that this affirming message was one He wanted me to share with others. As a victim of an abusive relationship, sometimes you feel like a different person. But you're not. *You're still you, the person God loves and others love too.*

Why Share?

What happened to me was deeply personal, deeply unsettling, deeply private. No one—*absolutely* **no one**—should have to experience what happened to me during my high school years. That's why I'm sharing my story. I don't want another person to experience an abusive relationship, especially a young person who is learning to navigate relationships, developing their life path, and establishing their core beliefs. Not my son or daughter, not their friends, not their classmates, not their peers.

Nor do I want this to happen to your child, your child's friend or classmate, one of your other family members, your coworker, or your neighbor. My hope in sharing my story and additional information associated with abuse is that together we can stop much of this relationship abuse from occurring.

How Common Are Abusive Relationships?

The reality is that thousands of people suffer from abuse every day—and to illustrate just how common it is, here are some facts from my own personal story. I graduated in a high school class of more than 850 people. At that time, I thought I was the only one in my class who was in an abusive relationship. But if I were to look at a high school group of that same size in light of today's statistics, 140 other students in that class would have suffered an abusive relationship.[1] And that's just taking into account the graduating class from *one* high school. In *one* town.

At the time of the abuse, I struggled alone. Clearly, so were others in my graduating class, but I didn't know about the pain they too were experiencing! It's tragic that so many people are not only victims of abuse but also usually struggle alone.

And this example is just focusing on the victims. The perpetrators are also negatively affected by their choices and actions, and they need help too but often don't receive it.

Abusive relationships can be hard to identify, and usually both the abuser and the victim work to hide them. It's my hope that the information offered in this book will not only help victims understand that abuse isn't their fault but also equip others—including mothers, fathers, teachers, youth directors, and other adults—to recognize the warning signs in order to help today's youth avoid getting into and staying in harmful relationships.

Why Stay?

It may be hard to understand why I stayed and why others stay in an abusive relationship. You may wonder, *Why don't they just leave?* or *Why did she stay for three years?* In the following chapters, I'll share with you

- how an abusive relationship starts subtly, then builds;
- why the person being abused stays; and
- indicators that can help victims as well as friends, parents, teachers, and others who work with youth recognize the warning signs.

Through these insights, concerned adults can equip teens to recognize the warning signs to avoid unhealthy or abusive relationships and help those trapped in these relationships get out and receive the counseling they will need to heal. And if you are a teen or young adult in an abusive relationship, hopefully this information can help you gather the courage and strength to safely leave. I'll also identify some of the factors that influence a person to be abusive so that we can help prevent and stop the cycle of abuse.

Adolescence can be a confusing time. Our teens are surrounded by an onslaught of messages: do this, wear this, act like this, sleep with this person, try this drink or drug, have a smoke, make fun of someone on social media. All these messages can make it confusing for teens to know how to live their lives. If we're aware of how these negative influences confront and affect our children, we can equip them with the tools they need to navigate the world they live in and make positive, healthy choices.

In addition, our youth are trying to figure out who they are while trying to fit in with their friends and peers. This can make them vulnerable to succumbing to risky behaviors. Many make risky choices without realizing they're hurting themselves. Whether they show it through drinking, doing drugs, smoking, driving recklessly, developing an eating disorder, being physically intimate with multiple partners, getting pregnant, being in an unhealthy or abusive relationship, or committing suicide, they're struggling and crying out for help. The scars they're creating could take years, sometimes decades, and for some, their entire lives to overcome.

I truly believe it takes a village to raise a child. My hope is that we can build a village where we work together to support our children and the communities we live in, where we provide positive experiences and role models rather than allowing the world to negatively affect and influence our children. Most importantly, I hope we build a village built in God's love.

Dee Dee Said
June 2022

PART ONE

MY TEENAGE
ABUSE STORY

Chapter 1
"Will a boy ever like me?"
Beginning to Date

I grew up in a military family—my dad was an officer in the air force, and my mom was a kindergarten teacher. I doted on my younger sister when she was an infant and toddler. Growing up we could push each other's buttons, but as we got older, most of the time we were good friends and hung out together. My family and I lived in six states before moving to Texas when I was thirteen.

In Arizona, where we lived before moving to Texas, our family often did activities together, from helping set up my mom's school classroom and enjoying activities at church, to camping or spending time with close family friends. Once we moved to Texas, we also started sailing on the weekends, often inviting a friend or two to join us.

My family attended Methodist churches. In Arizona, I was very involved in the youth group and spent most of the day each Sunday at the church with the youth. I loved learning about God and continued participating in youth group activities when we moved to Texas.

I tended to be shy, and it could be hard for me to make friends when we moved somewhere new. Thankfully, when we moved to Texas my mom knew another military family in the area with a daughter my age. The two moms arranged a get-together for me to meet several girls who were also in the seventh grade. So, by fall semester of eighth grade, I had a core group of good friends, both girls and guys.

In high school, I was a well-rounded student, earning mostly As and Bs, playing tennis on our high school's team, and becoming a member of the student council, the National Honor Society, and the local Rotary Club. I also enjoyed other normal teenage activities, like hanging out with friends, going to football games, having sleepovers with my girlfriends, and talking about boys.

By the time I entered high school, some of the friendships in my core "group" had turned into dating relationships. Although none of these relationships became serious or lasted more than a few months, by the beginning of my junior year I was the only one of my group of friends who hadn't been on a date. I longed for a boyfriend and wondered why not one boy at high school seemed interested in me. I grew insecure and worried if a boy would ever like me.

In the fall of my junior year, some friends and I were leaving school when a classmate asked me for a ride home.

When I answered yes, a friend of his, Brock (not his real name), also a junior at our school, jumped into my car too.

Within a few minutes, Brock started flirting with me. I flirted back, and when I dropped him off, he asked for my phone number. I eagerly gave it to him. Soon he began calling me, and we spent the next few weeks talking frequently on the phone.

Then during a phone call one evening, Brock asked me on a date. I told him I wasn't available on the night he'd asked about. Ironically, although I had spent years waiting to be asked on a date, a boy I played tennis with had invited me out to dinner on the same night.

Brock wanted to know why I wasn't available, and I tactfully explained I already had plans. He wanted to know with whom, so I told him. But when Brock, who was white, realized the other boy was Hispanic, he immediately responded with many racist and derogatory insults about the other boy. He also called me offensive names for even going out with the other boy.

I wish I'd had the Bible verse below tucked in my heart back then. What perfect advice it would have been:

> *Do not make friends with a hot-tempered person, do not associate with one easily angered, or you may learn their ways and get yourself ensnared.*
>
> (Proverbs 22:24–25)

When I hung up that evening, I was upset and a little shaken. I hadn't experienced someone talking to me like that before, and I didn't want to talk to Brock again. I kept my date with the other boy and had a good time, but while he and I remained friendly in school, he didn't ask me out again.

I didn't share with my mom why I had stopped talking to Brock, and she never asked, but about a week after the last phone call with him, my mom approached me. She told me that while Brock "might not look like Prince Charming," maybe I should go out with him. I didn't ask her why she felt I should date him, but I thought about her comment, and soon after that conversation, I started talking to Brock again.

He seemed once again like the nice person I'd started to get to know, and so after a few conversations, when he again asked me out on a date, I said yes.

My date with Brock was exactly what I thought a date was supposed to be like. When he arrived at my house, he came to the door to pick me up and meet my parents. After taking me out for dinner, he brought me home on time and walked me to my front door. I appreciated his chivalry and had enjoyed the date.

We saw each other frequently after that—hanging out after school, going to a haunted house with my friends, hiking and camping with the Rotary Club, double dating with one of his friends. The two of us were having fun together, and I was excited to finally have a boyfriend.

What's Going On?

Dating can be a significant factor in the lives of many adolescents. ACT for Youth Center of Excellence states, "Romantic relationships are central to social life during middle and late adolescence (ages 15–19)."[1] When it feels like everyone around you is dating, but you're not, it's easy to put pressure on yourself.

- Twenty-four percent of teens (ages sixteen to eighteen) said they feel pressure to have a boyfriend or girlfriend.[2]
- Results of studies vary, finding that between 35 percent to 72 percent of teens have dated.[3]

What Can We Do?

Beginning when our children are in elementary school and continuing through their middle and high school years, we can ask questions about the nature and temperament of their friendships. Often, we ask about their day and what they learned in school. Many of us might ask if others treat them "nicely." It's important also to describe to a child what "nice" behavior looks like; to inquire about their friends' other qualities, such as whether they are patient, kind, and respectful or sarcastic and superior; and to take the time to describe these character traits.

> If we start having character trait conversations early with our children and discuss what it means to treat others kindly and respectfully, they'll be more apt to recognize unhealthy behaviors as they get older.

Especially as our youth begin to date, we need to recognize that it's important to continue to expand on these conversations. For instance, we should start asking our teenagers what the people they're dating do to show that they care for and respect our teens. We should also ask our teenagers if they ever feel pressured by their dating partners to do things they don't want to do, such as going out on a particular evening or doing a specific activity, or if our children ever observe the other person saying unkind things about others or treating others poorly. Likewise, it's also important to ask our children what they do to show others they care for and respect them in return.

Chapter 2

"Can't you take a joke?"
Emotional Abuse

One day after school, Brock and my best friend, Linda, and I went to my house to hang out. Once we got there, Brock asked if we could go back to my bedroom, just to see what it looked like.

I wasn't supposed to have boys in my bedroom, especially when my parents weren't home. But I didn't want Brock to think I was a baby. Rather than speaking up and sticking to my parents' rule, I gave in to concerns about what he thought of me and took Brock and Linda to my room.

After hanging out for a few minutes in my room, Brock started play-wrestling with Linda and me. He kept wrapping his arms around us and either throwing us on the bed or pinning us down on it. With my limited experience, I thought this was a form of flirting and an excuse to get close to each other. I thought he was just doing it in fun—I was even a little jealous that he was playing with my friend this way too.

What's Going On?

Play-wrestling among people can actually be a warning sign of an abusive relationship. As licensed professional counselor Celeste Inman shares:

> Play-wrestling can be a red flag because it's a way the abuser can feel dominance over their partner. They make it look more playful so it's not as obvious; it can be calculated, a form of manipulation, or can also be a way of grooming to get their partner's guard down bit by bit. Not all play-wrestling indicates that the relationship will become abusive. Some possible red flags are if you ask them to stop and they don't, or if it causes pain and they continue.[1]

A few weeks into our relationship, Brock called me just before bedtime one night. He told me he'd been driving his dad's truck and had flipped it, totaling the truck. I was worried he might have been hurt in the accident, and I didn't think to ask how he'd gotten home. After assuring me he was okay, Brock asked me to stay on the phone with him, saying his dad was in the house and "really mad" at him. He told me his dad was so upset that Brock was worried he might hurt him, but that if we stayed on the phone, his dad would probably leave him alone.

As a naïve sixteen-year-old, I wanted to help him, so I buried myself under the covers and began talking quietly so my parents wouldn't know I was still on the phone. I talked with him for hours, and it never crossed my mind that if his dad was really upset, all he had to do was say, "Get off the phone!" and Brock would've had to hang up.

As the night wore on, I grew tired. But whenever I suggested it might be time to end the call, Brock would oppose the idea, either telling me his dad was still up or giving me another excuse to keep me on the phone. So, even though it was a school night, we talked until about 3:00 in the morning.

I arrived at school exhausted the next day and was surprised to find that Brock wasn't there. I grew terrified his dad had done something really bad to him. I wanted to help him. I told my best friend, but it never crossed my mind to tell a teacher or another adult. I couldn't check on Brock until I could get to one of the two pay phones on campus (this was before cell phones). Finally, during lunch period, I was able to use one of the phones. I had been concerned about Brock all morning, and my fears intensified when I called his house and no one answered the phone.

I was worried sick for the rest of the school day. After school my best friend and I drove straight to his house to check on him. As we turned onto his street, the first thing we saw was his dad's truck. It was sitting in the driveway—without a scratch on it.

At first, I was in disbelief and didn't know what to think. I had been worried about him all day, but now it appeared everything he'd told me the night before was a lie. As this realization dawned on me, I became both hurt and angry.

As I approached his front door, I heard his mom yell, "You're in trouble!" I was confused and wondered what was going on. When Brock came to the door, he was laughing—laughing so hard he fell through the open screen door. For a minute I just stood there in disbelief. I started asking questions, trying to comprehend that he hadn't been in an accident and asking why he hadn't been at school. He continued laughing at me, making fun of me for how gullible I'd been the night before. I felt upset and stupid for believing his lies. I tried to tell him it was wrong to have lied to me, but he started telling me it was "just a joke." He even pushed the situation back on me, saying, "Can't you take a joke?"

I was torn. While what he had done didn't feel right, I also didn't know if it was something worth breaking up over. In my mind, I started debating whether his "joke" was worth not having a boyfriend. The truth was, having a boyfriend made me feel more accepted, and I needed that at the time.

Looking back, I realize this nonjoke was the beginning of Brock's mind games. It was the beginning of his emotional control over me.

In addition to lying to me, Brock began to reveal a different attitude toward my friends and family. At the beginning of our relationship, he was nice to my friends, and we frequently hung out with them. But soon Brock began to talk negatively to me about the people in my life. He made derogatory comments about my friends and made fun of my parents and sister. None of what he said was true (and I'd rather not repeat what he said here), but he clearly didn't find them worthy, so I withdrew from others. In an effort to please him, I spent less and less time with my friends and family because I thought my association with them would affect his feelings for me.

Brock didn't stop at devaluing my friends and family—he started putting me down too. He regularly pointed out so many flaws in me that I stopped believing in my abilities. For example, even though I took harder classes in school than Brock did (he was in some remedial classes), he would frequently make fun of me, saying, "It's better to have common sense than book sense." He pointed out, "Nothing you're learning in books helps you with decisions that need to be made in the real world." He would laugh and tell me how dumb I was because he thought I lacked common sense. He always asserted himself as superior to me, and I began to feel very insecure.

Brock put me down in areas besides academics. After watching me at tennis practice one day, he told me, "You don't have any coordination! No wonder you can't play well." When he made comments like this, he usually added, "I'm only kidding. Can't you take a joke?" He also pointed out flaws in my physical appearance, saying, "You're lucky to have me. No one else would want you." I began to question how other people could like me as a friend, let alone romantically.

What's Going On?

Emotional abuse is a pattern of behavior in which the abuser insults or humiliates their partner to isolate, control, or frighten them. The victim may begin to doubt themselves and develop a distorted self-esteem and self-worth.[2]

At the beginning of a romantic relationship, the abuser is often nice, charming, attentive, and/or thoughtful. The emotional abuse starts gradually and builds; often, it's so subtle the victim doesn't realize it's occurring. Some victims speak up as the abuser begins to make derogatory comments, but the abuser dismisses the victim's rebuttals and continues with the insults, leading the victim to start doubting the worthiness of their perceptions, their feelings, and ultimately themselves.

As the relationship begins to feel uncomfortable, the victim thinks they're the root of the problem, and they start trying very hard to "fix" the relationship, to bring it back to what it was in the beginning.

Most often, the victim doesn't see the emotional abuse until they're out of the relationship. Instead, as it's happening, they doubt themselves and believe what the abuser says about them, as the abuser is systematically breaking down their self-confidence over time.

It's often difficult to recognize if someone you know is involved in a relationship characterized by verbal and/or emotional abuse, and it's extremely difficult for the people on the receiving end of the abuse to recognize it as well. Both forms of abuse can be hard to recognize for several reasons:

- It can be subtle.
- There is a lack of physical signs of abuse.
- Teens with limited dating experience may believe it's a normal part of relationships.[3]

Another reason it can be hard to recognize a growing relationship is unhealthy is that, as a society, **we're desensitized to emotional abuse**. It surrounds us—from "playful" sarcasm or bullying in school to song lyrics that put others down and television shows that portray unhealthy, even emotionally abusive relationships.[4] Let me illustrate using one of my own experiences:

When I was a teenager, I loved watching the TV sitcom *Growing Pains*. At first sight, it's a great family show about an intact, traditional, and affluent family. The parents are married, with three kids and a dog. Both parents are involved with their kids, and the dad seems like a good role model. The oldest son is quite mischievous, and the dad tries to share his wisdom with him.

Yet there is an undercurrent of emotional abuse in the family that is disguised as "comedy." The middle child, Carol Seaver, excels in school, and as a result, her two brothers regularly make fun of her. They put her down for being smart, ridicule her appearance, and frequently make fat jokes about her. The brothers often laugh and congratulate each other when they deliver a particularly good put-down to Carol.

As much as I thought I loved the show, it was confusing to me. I liked Carol and identified with her. I didn't understand why the dad, who was a psychiatrist on the show, tolerated how his sons treated his daughter. Occasionally the dad would yell "Mike!" or attempt to lecture his oldest son. But rather than experiencing consequences, Mike frequently got away with his pranks and disrespectful behavior. Whenever Carol was ridiculed, I winced. It was "comedy" at someone else's expense.

Once I was an adult, it didn't surprise me to read that the *Growing Pains* storyline had real-life consequences for Tracey Gold, the actress who portrayed Carol Seaver. A *Daily Beast* article based on an interview with Gold shared:

> She [Tracey Gold] had struggled with food her entire life, but among the things that put her over the edge were the fat jokes targeted at her character [Carol Seaver]. She recalls sitting at script readings, pleading with the writers to cut the nastier lines (they countered with, "But it's

funny!"). "I think the fat jokes did a disservice to young girls in America because I was never fat," Gold says. "It was really hurting my feelings. It wasn't about Carol Seaver. If you're making fun of Carol Seaver's body, you're making fun of Tracey's body. It was a personal kind of thing at a vulnerable age. I didn't know how to really process that." [5]

For the next twenty years of her life, Tracey Gold battled eating disorders. At times her disease was life-threatening, as her weight dipped as low as eighty pounds.

Ridicule, sarcasm, and insulting comments shouldn't be used for humor on TV, and it's not how we should treat each other in real life. **Emotional and psychological abuse can be detrimental to self-esteem.** Other short- and long-term consequences are detailed in the following lists.

Unfortunately, too many of us have learned that this ridicule style of "humor" is not only tolerated but acceptable. The truth is that abuse of any kind shouldn't be condoned or endured.

A relationship can be verbally or emotionally abusive without becoming physically abusive. One of the warning signs of an abusive relationship is being put down. Unfortunately, a staggering number of tweens have experienced negative remarks from their dating partners. Sixty-two percent of tweens surveyed said they knew friends who had been verbally abused (called "stupid," "worthless," "ugly," etc.) by a boyfriend or girlfriend.[6]

Below, and on the next two pages, is information regarding verbal and emotional abuse as well as components of healthy relationships.[7]

Verbal Abuse Red Flags:
- Name-calling
- Put-downs
- Yelling or shouting
- Threatening the partner or one of the partner's family members

Psychological/Emotional Abuse Red Flags:
- Ignoring a date's feelings
- Insulting a date's beliefs or values
- Acting in an intimidating way
- Calling a date names
- Using sexually derogatory names
- Isolating a date from others
- Driving recklessly to scare a date
- Displaying inappropriate anger
- Damaging personal property
- Putting down a date's family and friends
- Humiliating a date in public or private
- Telling lies

The effects of emotional abuse are both immediate and lasting. In fact, these effects are often more damaging to the victim's mental health than physical abuse.

Short-term effects of emotional abuse:

- Surprise and confusion
- Shame or guilt
- Becoming overly passive or compliant
- Frequent crying
- Avoidance of eye contact
- Feeling undesirable
- Feeling powerless and defeated, because nothing you do ever seems to be right (learned helplessness)
- Feeling like you are "walking on eggshells"
- Anxiety or fear; hypervigilance

Long-term effects of emotional abuse:

- Depression
- Withdrawal
- Low self-esteem and self-worth
- Emotional instability
- Sleep disturbances
- Chronic anxiety
- Physical pain without a cause
- Suicidal ideation, thoughts, or attempts
- Extreme dependence on the abuser

- Underachievement
- Inability to trust
- Feeling trapped and alone
- Substance abuse

What Can We Do?

Many teens and tweens today don't understand what characterizes a healthy relationship because it may not be present in their home (their parents may be single, divorced, or married but in a poor relationship) or simply because they're new to or inexperienced at dating.

It's important that we as adults—whether we're parents, teachers, other family members, neighbors, or youth directors—model and/or explain to the youth and adolescents around us that healthy relationships include the following:

- Mutual respect
- Trust
- Consideration
- Kindness
- Honesty
- Good communication

If we discuss the characteristics of healthy versus harmful relationships often and consistently with the youth in our lives, we can help them learn to recognize the warning signs should they, or one of their friends, encounter someone who is verbally or emotionally abusive.

Learning these skills and being able to identify whether they're present in a youth's dating relationship can make a profound difference in their life and protect them from damaging relationships.

Chapter 3

"If you loved me, you would!"
Sexual Coercion

As Brock and I began dating, I wanted to be kissed and have my hand held. I wanted him to put his arm around me when we watched a scary movie. Although I had seen relationships progress quickly on TV, it didn't cross my mind that our relationship would progress beyond my expectations.

Several weeks after we started dating, Brock and I went hiking with the local Rotary group at a state park a couple of hours out of town. Our group met in the morning and carpooled to the park. It was a beautiful fall day, and Brock and I had a great time hiking and having fun together. After returning to town that evening, we picked up a movie and went back to his house to watch it.

When we got there, the house was dark, with only a single, dim light on in the whole house. Brock's parents had already gone to bed, so he and I were in the family room alone. The two of us sat on the couch and started to watch the movie. Soon he lay down on the couch and suggested I lie beside him.

I was uncomfortable with the idea, but once again I didn't want him to think I was a baby, so I did as he asked and lay next to him in a spooning position. Brock draped his arm across my arm and chest as we continued to watch the movie.

After a while Brock rolled me toward him so we were facing each other and started kissing me. Then his hands started moving over my body to areas I wasn't ready for him to touch. After a while he started unbuttoning my shirt and trying to unbutton my pants. I didn't know what to do—I wanted a relationship, and I wanted him to hold my hand, put his arm around my shoulder, and kiss me a little—but I wasn't ready for this!

On the other hand, I wanted Brock to like me, and I didn't want him to think I was immature, so I continued to kiss him and let him touch me. Although I had seen many intimate situations on TV shows, I didn't know how to handle them myself in real life. I didn't know I needed to set limits with Brock, much less where to set them. I did stop him before things went too far, but that night marked the beginning of sexual pressure.

From that point on, Brock kept pressuring me physically. Anytime we were alone and kissing, he continued trying to touch my chest, push his hands inside my pants, unbutton my shirt, or unzip my pants.

Within a few weeks, he was pressuring me to have sex with him. And not just sometimes—always. He began saying things like, "It's a way to show each other we care." "We're exclusive, so why not?" and "What's the big deal?" Soon it progressed to "If you loved me, you would."

These comments and activities were unsettling. I knew God made sex to be something special to be shared between two people once they were married. I didn't want to have sex with someone who wasn't my husband or at such a young age, but I also wasn't prepared for someone to push me toward it so persistently or so relentlessly. I told Brock no, but the coercion was always there.

Unfortunately, it never crossed my mind that his behavior was unacceptable. It also never crossed my mind that other guys at my high school might not pressure me to be intimate with them, and instead might respect and support my decision to wait. At the time, I thought Brock was acting in ways characteristic of our peers, and that every guy pressured his girlfriend—after all, I'd seen that kind of behavior a million times on TV and in movies.

So, as much as I didn't like it, it became routine to kiss Brock, and then for him to test and ridicule the sexual limits I set. I constantly had to hold him back from going too far. I didn't realize battling my boyfriend emotionally and sexually wasn't part of a healthy relationship. I thought it was just part of dating.

Part of the problem was that at Brock's house his parents allowed us to be together in his bedroom with the door closed. They even assumed we were having sex!

After dating for a few months, Brock and I were in his bedroom one afternoon with the door closed. I was having the usual struggle with him—Brock kissing me, his hands traveling, buttons and zippers being undone—and as usual, I kept trying to appease him while not allowing things to go too far. I was uncomfortable with how far we had progressed, but Brock was always pushing to go even further.

This day, we were kissing while half sitting, half lying on his bed. We weren't naked, but clothes were undone and body parts were exposed. As we were kissing, I felt something enter my vagina, and I immediately pulled away and back from Brock. He looked at me and told me we'd just had sex. I was mortified, stunned, hurt, and angry.

I was ashamed that I'd had sex and hadn't waited for marriage. I felt somewhat numb.

After that day, Brock became more persistent in pushing me to have sex again, saying things like, "We already had sex. What's the big deal?" But I wouldn't agree to have sex with him.

After about two weeks, Brock admitted that he'd lied, explaining it had actually been his finger that had entered me. He told me he was hoping that if I believed I was no longer a virgin I wouldn't resist him anymore.

I was hurt and angry that he'd lied, but I still didn't think about breaking up with him. It seemed like everyone at school was dating, and there were rumors of other couples having sex. I liked being part of a couple and continued to assume any relationship would be like this.

About a month later, I did give in to Brock's ongoing, consistent pressure to have sex. Afterward, I was very upset that things had progressed to that level, but I also believed it was my fault for giving in. I blamed myself and not him.

Once Brock had coerced me into having sex, I felt ashamed, guilty, and alone. I believed premarital sex was wrong for me and didn't admit to anyone that I had become sexually active. I knew my parents wouldn't approve, and I didn't think they'd understand, so I felt I couldn't talk to them about it. Because I was ashamed, I also didn't want to confide in my friends.

Deep in my soul I knew that God meant for each of us to become intimate with only one person—and so at this time I made up my mind that Brock was the person I was going to marry and with whom I would spend the rest of my life.

Still, betraying my faith by sleeping with Brock affected me deeply. I began to withdraw from church. I felt like a hypocrite sitting in the pews on Sunday morning, and soon I made excuses to skip youth group before quitting the group altogether. As my sexual relationship with Brock continued, I was relieved on the weeks my family missed church.

What's Going On?

Our kids' encounters with sexual activity and pressure related to sex can start at a young age.

- Some children start dating at young ages. This means they're also exploring actions that come with dating, including holding hands, kissing, and even having sex.
- Thirty-seven percent of tweens (eleven- to fourteen-year-olds) say touching and feeling up is part of a dating relationship.[1]
- In a 2019 survey of high school students, 38.4 percent had engaged in sexual intercourse.[2] The number of teens becoming sexually active increases with each year, from 20 percent at age fifteen to 48 percent at age seventeen.[3]
- Thirty-five percent of boys and 28 percent of girls ages fifteen to seventeen have had oral sex. By the time they're eighteen to nineteen years old, 65 percent of boys and 61 percent of girls have engaged in oral sex.[4]
- One-third of teen boys feel peer pressured into becoming sexually active.[5]

Many teenage boys aren't ready for physically intimate relationships any more than girls are, but because they feel pressure from their peers, and there are social and media influences to become sexually active, they in turn pressure their female partners.[6] In recent years, girls in high school and college have begun to feel this same pressure and may flirt suggestively or be just as aggressive as boys are in applying pressure on their dates to have sex.

The pressure comes in several forms. High-school-age and college-age boys are apt to share stories with friends and acquaintances of everything from having sex with their partner to how they coerced a partner. Many TV shows and movies portray storylines of sexually active teens or sexually coercive behavior. Often, teens don't understand that pressuring another or using these tactics is wrong.

Coercion is a tactic many use to gain what they want from someone else, from a classmate bullying a peer for lunch money to an executive applying pressure in a business deal. In a dating relationship, sometimes one partner may exert pressure in the pursuit of sex. When an individual experiences *sexual coercion*, they are being pressured to do something sexually or physically that they are not comfortable doing. The person on the receiving end may give in to the coercion for any number of reasons, afterward feeling guilt and shame.

In order to get their way and "do what everyone else is doing," teenagers may use the following tactics to lower their partner's sexual resistance or force someone to have sex with them:[7]

- Sixty-three percent get angry or make the other person feel guilty. For example, they'll say, "What do you mean you won't have sex with me? You kissed me and led me on. You're a tease!" or "If you loved/ cared about me, you would."
- Thirty-two percent argue or pressure the person. For example, they'll say, "We're exclusive, and having sex is part of a dating relationship." Or they might agree to setting sexual boundaries but later push their partner to go further.
- Fifteen percent use alcohol to lower their partner's resistance. Some may encourage their partner to drink, while others may add alcohol to a drink without the other person knowing or add more alcohol than the victim is aware of.
- Eight percent use physical force, such as holding the other person down.
- Five percent intimidate. The abuser may threaten to tell others that the couple has been sexually active, spread rumors about the activity they've engaged in—when they haven't actually had sex—or physically threaten to harm the other person if they don't agree to have sex.

It's common for youth to experience sexual coercion, as studies confirm:

- Twenty-nine percent of girls who have been in a relationship said they've been pressured to have sex or to engage in sexual activity when they didn't want to do so.[8]
- Twenty-three percent of girls reported they've gone further sexually in a relationship than they wanted.[9]
- Forty-five percent of girls know a friend or peer who has felt pressured into having either intercourse or oral sex.[10]
- Data from the 2015 national Youth Risk Behavior Survey of ninth- through twelfth-grade students found that 10 percent of females and 3 percent of males have experienced forced sex.[11]

The pressure to have sex places many teens in disturbing and harmful situations, such as consuming too much alcohol or becoming a victim of date rape. Other consequences of teen sex include sexually transmitted diseases (STDs) and teen pregnancies. Even more crucial is the emotional toll having sex can have on our children:

- WebMD reports, "Many sexually active teens have felt used or felt bad about themselves post-sex."[12]
- The Heritage Foundation reports, "When compared with teens that abstain from sexual activity, those

that are sexually active were less likely to report feelings of happiness and more likely to exhibit signs of depression."[13]

- Sexual activity places adolescents at risk of HIV infection, other STDs, and unintended pregnancy.[14]
- Teens and young adults ages fifteen to twenty-four account for half of new cases of STDs annually.[15] Having an STD can be very upsetting to a teen, especially if they don't feel they can confide in anyone about their symptoms or aren't able to access medical help.

What Can We Do?

As adults and parents, we need to understand the pressure and sexual coercion that confront our children—both our daughters and our sons. It's hard enough for adults to discern values in today's society, but it's even harder for adolescents who are just beginning to explore the world of relationships.

Although some children may be inexperienced and naïve, others are not and will try to use this to their advantage. Many adolescents will be pressured for sex, whether it comes from someone with harmful intentions or a teen wanting to keep up with others. Our children need us to talk with them and provide them with the knowledge to avoid harmful situations. We also need to help them know how to say no and walk away from bad situations.

In any dating relationship, pressure for sex is never acceptable. We need to give our children—again, both our daughters and our sons—the tools to make good decisions about sexual purity. We shouldn't just tell them they should wait for marriage before becoming intimate, but inform them *why* it's important to wait, including these points:[16]

- How we date influences what our marriage will be like. Strong relationships are based on mutual respect, spending time together, and sharing and listening to each other's thoughts and feelings.
- Having multiple partners before marriage may make it harder to be monogamous once married.
- Physical intimacy creates a tighter bond, which is a good thing inside a marriage; but when introduced while dating, it can make it harder to discern red flags or determine whether the relationship is right for them.
- If a couple breaks up, it's harder to get over each other than if they had not been physically intimate.
- Being sexually active puts them at risk of contracting STDs, including HPV, and increases their risk of developing certain types of cancer.
- Being sexually active entails the risk of becoming pregnant.

- Individuals who wait until they're married to have sex rate their relationship stability, satisfaction, and physical intimacy higher than those who did not wait.

We also need to help teens understand how, in the real world, to say no and walk away from bad situations without feeling ashamed, embarrassed, insecure, or guilty. We can help them develop self-confidence in this area by discussing the following:

- Decide what you want before you're in a relationship or intimate situation.
- Your values are your values. Not everyone has to agree with them, and that's okay. But they're yours and worth maintaining—don't compromise on them.
- Regardless of how great the person is in other ways, if the two of you have different core values, they're most likely not the person for you.
- It's okay—actually, more than okay—to stand up for yourself and say no to something you don't want to do.
- You never owe someone an explanation when your answer is no. Not wanting to do something is all the reason you need.
- Many teens are worried that their dating partner may break up with them if they don't have sex. But if the other person doesn't respect your values, they are

not the right person for you, and the relationship won't work out in the long term.

- Believe in yourself. It's important to know who you are, stand up for yourself, and walk away from the relationship if you feel compromised in any way.

Here are some tips for saying no in a way that will make the teen feel more confident:

- Standing or sitting up tall gives us confidence and helps us breathe better, which can help us collect our thoughts.
- Looking the other person in the eye while saying no indicates confidence. Even if we don't feel strong on the inside, we appear so on the outside.
- Slouching and/or looking away can make us feel unsure of ourselves, even defeated.

Below is a list from the B4UDecide website (used with permission) of common phrases one person may use to pressure another to have sex, as well as suggestions for resisting them.[17] Discussing this list with your teen can help them prepare rebuttals for potential situations in which they feel pressured for sex.

Why won't you have sex with me?

- I don't want to, and I don't have to give you a reason why.

We've done it before—what's the problem now?

- Just because I've had sex before doesn't mean I can't decide not to now.
- I realized that I'm actually not ready. It's got nothing to do with you.
- I just want to make sure that I'm completely ready the next time.

You told me you're not a virgin—why would you sleep with someone else but not me?

- I may not be a virgin, but that doesn't mean I sleep around.
- That time was a mistake.
- Just because I've had sex before doesn't mean I can't decide not to now.
- I've decided that I want to wait until I'm older before I have sex again. It's not that big a deal.

But I love you—don't you love me?

- I do love you . . . and I would think that if you loved me, you wouldn't pressure me into a choice I'm not ready to make.
- If you loved me, you wouldn't try to pressure me like this.

- I'm just not ready—I want this to mean something,
  and I feel like we need to take it more slowly.

Are you afraid?

- Yes, and you should be too. What if I/you got
  pregnant?

If you don't sleep with me, I'll find someone else who will.

- Off you go, then.
- If that's what it's all about to you, then I'm not that
  interested in you anymore.

I'd hate to have to cheat on you—I really love you, but I have needs. If I can't have sex with you, I'll have to find some other way to get what I need.

- If you loved me, you wouldn't mind waiting until I was
  ready. You're not going to explode if we don't have
  sex.

Are you frigid? It's not normal not to have sex.

- It's not normal to pressure someone into having sex.

You're just a tease.

- What are you talking about? Kissing you doesn't
  mean I want to have sex with you.
- Sex is a big step, and I'm not doing it until I'm
  completely sure. I don't care what you call me.

It's also extremely helpful to educate and encourage our children to think about ways to avoid tempting situations and keep themselves safe when they don't want to engage in an activity—any activity, whether sexual or otherwise. Below are a few examples:

- A youth director I spoke with shared that when he and his (now) wife were dating in college, they agreed to limit alone time together (i.e., they intentionally avoided being alone in cars, apartments, etc.). Instead, they went on double dates and hung out with friends, and went to restaurants or other public places. High school students can also be at public places, restaurants, or each other's or friends' houses, especially when parents with rules are home.

- Teens can choose constructive activities together as their "dates," whether studying together or in groups at the library; participating in a school, church, or other activity; or volunteering together. There are lots of options.

- They should always have their cell phone with them and be sure to charge it before going out.

- Always let them know they can call you anytime and you'll pick them up, no questions asked. It's also helpful to have a prearranged signal or phrase they can use to indicate they're asking for help (such as "I forgot to walk the dog before I left"). This way if the person they're with sees the message, they won't know the true meaning or make fun of your teen for wanting to leave.

- When going on a date or meeting up with a group of teens, they should have money with them or an alternate means of transportation if they are riding with a group.
- If they're ever in a situation where they don't feel safe, they should leave as soon as possible and move to a group setting or join up with people they trust.
- Have them practice saying no ahead of time with a parent, friend, sibling, or another trusted adult. Practicing like this will help build confidence, and they'll be better prepared should the need arise.
- Remind teens to refrain from trying alcohol or drugs, which comes with the risk of lowering resistance and decision-making skills. If alcohol or drugs are used, they also run the risk of being incapacitated and forced into something they don't want to do.

If we have these conversations with our tweens and teens, do you know what? The chances are quite good that our youth will listen to us! Teens surveyed share that *parents have the biggest influence on their decisions about sexual activity*.[18] Our kids want and need us to talk with them about friends, relationships, and sex, even though most are just as uncomfortable starting a conversation with us about these things as we may be with them.

While it may be uncomfortable, it's necessary to start and continue having conversations with our kids in order to educate and protect them. Once the conversations start, they're often not as hard as we anticipated.

Rather than wait, we should make the effort right now—today—to give our children the tools they need to say no and set limits. This is the best way to ensure that they understand that they could and should talk to us if they begin experiencing pressure from a boyfriend or girlfriend.

Chapter 4

"He didn't mean to hurt me.
It must have been an accident."
Denial

As our physical relationship started and progressed, Brock became jealous. At first, it seemed flattering. As an insecure teen, it was reassuring to hear that my boyfriend was jealous of another boy and worried about losing me to him.

Brock's jealousy started to show when I mentioned a conversation I had with another boy in class or a comment one of his friends had made as we crossed paths between classes. When I remarked on the exchange, Brock would immediately spew a barrage of questions and accusations. I would defend myself, and afterward he would apologize, saying, "I just love you so much and don't want to lose you."

Rather than recognize that his actions and jealousy weren't part of a healthy relationship, I believed that these things going on in our relationship were my fault. I started to question myself and wonder if maybe I shouldn't have talked to that other boy in class or said hi to Brock's friend in the hall. Jealousy was adding yet another tool to Brock's arsenal for controlling me.

Now that my boyfriend had worn me down emotionally and sexually, he began to abuse me physically. It started one day when we were talking to one of his friends in the hall after school. The three of us were debating something trivial. In an attempt to look cool in front of his friend, I playfully and lightly backhanded Brock's shoulder during our conversation. In return, he shoved me so hard that I fell to the floor, sliding backward and spilling my books.

I was embarrassed. Humiliated. Red flags went off in my mind, but I quickly denied their significance, telling myself I must be overreacting. He was bigger than me (I was five feet six and 100 pounds, and he was six feet and 180 pounds), so I told myself that he hadn't meant to push me that hard and that he wouldn't hurt me, especially in front of someone else. It must have been an accident, and I was the one who had started it by tapping his shoulder. So, at the time of the incident, all I did was scramble to collect myself and pick up my books. I was embarrassed to have been pushed that far and didn't share it with any of my friends. I didn't ask them what they thought or whether the action was okay. In fact, I didn't share this with anyone for twenty years.

What's Going On?

Denial plays a large role in an abusive dating relationship. Such relationships have four stages, constituting what's known as *battered woman syndrome*. The first stage is denial. Here's a description from the Laws.com website:

Denial occurs when victims of abuse cannot admit and acknowledge that they are being subjected to domestic violence. During this stage, a victim of intimate partner abuse will not only avoid admitting the abuse to their friends and their family members, but they themselves will not acknowledge the brutality that they are suffering from. They will fail to recognize that there are any problems between themselves and their partner. Multiple factors may contribute to a victim's unwavering denial.

In many instances, an individual does not realize that they are being subjected to domestic violence. This is largely due to the manipulative and coercive behavior of their abuser. The acts of abuse may be so covert that they do not appear to be harmful or detrimental. In other instances, a victim of domestic violence may believe that denial is the most effective way to avoid being subjected to further violence and brutality. Whatever the cause, denial is extremely adverse. Until a victim admits and confronts the abuse they are experiencing, they will not be able to provide themselves with the help and the protection they need.[1]

Many of us tend to associate violence in a relationship with domestic violence and therefore believe it's more likely to occur in adults who are married or living together. The hard reality is quite different. **Girls and young women ages sixteen to twenty-four actually experience the highest rates of intimate partner violence and sexual assault.**[2] Additionally, since children today start dating young, this kind of abuse can begin early. Studies show that children as young as eleven are victims of sexual violence, including rape, physical violence, psychological violence, or stalking.[3]

- Teen dating violence can affect anyone—both females and males, all races, and all social and economic groups.[4]
- Among women who have been in an abusive dating relationship, 45 percent experienced the first occurrence between the ages of eighteen and twenty-four. Twenty-six percent were under the age of eighteen.[5]

Abusive dating violence affects teens in numerous ways. When someone is being abused, there is an increased risk of

- substance use,
- unhealthy weight-control behaviors (such as anorexia or bulimia),
- sexual-risk behaviors (multiple partners, unprotected sex, etc.),
- pregnancy, and
- suicide.[6]

Even if our children, or the youth we know, are fortunate not to experience an abusive relationship, they could still be affected. In the proposal for H.R. 3297: Teen Dating Violence Education Act of 2013, Congress stated, "Forty percent of teenage girls ages 14 to 17 report knowing someone their age who has been hit or beaten by a boyfriend."[7]

As much as I hope none of our children will be affected by an abusive relationship, the reality is that too many of our children will suffer at the hands of another:

Approximately one in three adolescent girls will experience an abusive relationship.[8] In the majority of abusive dating relationships, girls and young women are the victims, but one in fourteen males is also abused.[9]

To put this into perspective, compare the number of people abused to breast cancer patients. One in eight women is at risk of developing breast cancer in her lifetime.[10] **Our girls are two and a half times more likely to experience an abusive dating relationship by the age of twenty-four than to develop breast cancer in their lifetime.**

What Can We Do?

As a society, we don't often talk about teen dating violence. Many of us may not know much about abusive teen dating relationships—how to prevent them, what to do, or where to go for help. This book (especially in part two) will give you those tools.

In the next few chapters, I'll share examples of physical abuse to provide a better understanding of what might be happening in the victim's relationship, and how the victim may be feeling.

Chapter 5

Dr. Jekyll and Mr. Hyde

Components of Physical Abuse

As Brock's physical abuse started, his emotional abuse intensified, with these two forms of maltreatment working in tandem to strengthen his control.

The play-wrestling we had engaged in early in our relationship took an extremely negative turn. Instead of wrestling with me flirtatiously, Brock said I had to learn about body pressure points in case I needed to defend myself during a physical attack by a stranger or an acquaintance. But instead of teaching me how to do these moves myself, Brock demonstrated *on me*. He applied just enough pressure for it to be painful while telling me he was only "lightly" applying pressure to the area between my neck and the top of my shoulder, and that with increased pressure, it would be easy to inflict immobilizing pain on me.

Brock's desire to inflict physical pain on me soon morphed into another form. Occasionally when the two of us were sitting someplace together, he would abruptly grab my arm and bite it very hard. Startled, I would scream out in pain and immediately try to pull my arm away.

Brock would release my arm within a few seconds. As he did so, he would laugh and say, "I just wondered what it would be like to eat a piece of someone—to take a bite out of them." Although he never bit me hard enough to break through the skin and draw blood, the bite usually left a bruise on my arm in the shape of his mouth, including teeth marks.

Such occurrences were always unexpected, quick to occur, and of course quite frightening. What I didn't understand at the time was that Brock was gradually working to instill fear in me on many levels.

For example, one day we went to his backyard to lift weights on his weight bench. Brock's large dog stayed outside unleashed, and so it was in the backyard with us.

I had seen the dog through the back door before but hadn't been around it much. Once Brock and I began working out, he told me the dog was "part wolf" and "could be vicious." At first, I laughed his statements off, thinking he was teasing me or giving me a hard time. But Brock kept talking about the dog's aggressive nature until eventually I got nervous being around it. All I wanted to do now was to bolt inside Brock's house and get away from the dog!

When I reached this point, it was as if Brock could read my mind. He looked at me and said matter-of-factly that the worst thing I could do was show fear because the dog could sense that and would attack me.

I was desperate to maintain a calm composure, but as Brock relentlessly continued with these comments, I got close to breaking down. I knew my fear must be apparent to the dog.

Although Brock was the one who sparked and fueled my fears, at the time I didn't recognize that. Instead, I felt I needed him to protect me and save me from the dog. As my fear grew, Brock once again began laughing at me before he went on to tell me "it's fine," that he'd just been teasing me. He then reassured me that everything was okay, and the dog wouldn't attack me.

This was a technique that Brock used so I would develop a false sense of security from being around him and would view him as my protector—when in reality I needed to be protected from *him*. Looking back, I realize Brock was the cause of my near hysteria. It was his way of gaining control in the situation and relationship while making me dependent on him.

Another day, I spoke to one of Brock's friends in the hallway between classes. When I mentioned the brief conversation to Brock later, he became upset and interrogated me. After he finished yelling and spitting angry questions at me, he calmed down and told me his response was *my* fault. If I hadn't acted inappropriately, he said, he wouldn't have reacted that way.

Although I understand now that Brock was the one creating these abusive situations (emotional, verbal, physical safety, etc.), at the time each and every occurrence felt like he was reacting to something *I* was doing wrong—meaning that I, and not Brock, was the cause.

Through this cycle of manipulation, control, and abuse, Brock made sure to convey many "rules" to me. Among other things, some of the rules he insisted on dictated how I could dress and whom I could and couldn't talk to. His rules were random and ever-changing; first I couldn't wear short skirts, then another time it was overalls. Most of the time his rules included not talking to other boys, but there were also a few girls he forbade me to hang out with.

Unfortunately, I usually learned of these rules only by crossing the line—a line I knew nothing about before I crossed it—and then suffering the consequences of having made a misstep. Brock would get extremely upset or jealous over something I'd done, and that's when I would discover I had talked to someone he didn't want me to talk to, looked at someone the "wrong way," or said the wrong thing to him. He would then get abusive toward me, yelling at me until I was in tears, pushing me backward or into a wall, and even hitting and punching me.

Then, all of a sudden, it would be over. It was as if a tornado had torn through our surroundings, and then everything became still and calm. Brock would hug me close or tenderly pull me onto his lap and say how much he loved me and that he never meant to hurt me. While holding me, he would say he was sorry—and that if I hadn't done "X," he wouldn't have gotten upset.

I felt like I was dating Dr. Jekyll and Mr. Hyde. If I acted the way he wanted, being careful not to say or do the wrong thing, I had a nice and loving boyfriend. But if I accidentally did the wrong thing, I had to survive until the monster's rage subsided and my boyfriend returned.

What's Going On?

Abusive relationships involve a never-ending cycle of control. In this cycle, one partner is abusive, then "saves" the other person from being hurt, and so the person being victimized starts depending on them for "safety." The irony is that the abuser is the one causing the harm.

Usually, by the time personal safety is a concern, the victim's self-esteem has already been diminished through ridicule and derogatory comments. The abused partner doubts their own abilities while simultaneously developing an unhealthy trust in the other person.

What Can Make a Person Abusive?

Sometimes a person abuses another because they have been abused themselves. A few times during our relationship, Brock made comments that led me to believe his dad had been physically abusive with him in the past, as well as emotionally abusive with his mom. Rather than flee, I felt sympathetic and wanted to help him.

Coming from an abusive home is not the only reason individuals abuse. Lundy Bancroft, former co-director of Emerge, the nation's first program for abusive men, has worked with abusive men for over seventeen years. In his book *Why Does He DO That?* Bancroft shares that more than half of his clients do *not* come from abusive homes. **Exposure to cultural influences, such as a child's neighborhood, television shows, books, jokes, songs, and role models, is sufficient to teach a child to become an abusive person.**[1] In fact, numerous studies have found that exposure to violent video games correlates with aggression in the real world.[2]

Emotionally and physically abusive messages surround our children today—not just in the video games they play, but also in the television shows and movies they watch, the songs they listen to, and the jokes they hear. So, a child can grow up in a healthy home environment with loving parents, relatives, and friends but learn negative behavior from the influences around them.

Likewise, many men who grow up in abusive homes have chosen to stop their family's cycle of abuse, rather than repeat it, by leading nonviolent lives. The example set by such people shows that the circumstances within a child's family are only part of the picture. A child exposed to alternative thoughts and actions can choose positive behaviors instead of abusive behavior.[3]

As for the factors that increase the risk that someone will physically harm their dating partner, the Centers for Disease Control and Prevention (CDC) cites the following traits and situations:[4]

- Being more depressed and more aggressive than their peers
- Exhibiting problem behaviors in other areas
- Using alcohol
- Experiencing symptoms of trauma
- Having a friend involved in dating violence
- Believing that dating violence is acceptable
- Being or having been exposed to harsh parenting
- Being or having been exposed to inconsistent discipline
- Experiencing a lack of parental supervision, monitoring, or warmth

What Can We Do?

Our children need healthy boundaries and positive influences so they can choose healthy behavior and avoid harmful relationships. Thankfully, there are things we can do to help ensure that our children have positive influences. A report by the Surgeon General cites the presence of the following factors that help *prevent* teens from becoming perpetrators of violence:[5]

- Parental monitoring
- Engagement in school academics and activities
- The perception that there will be penalties for doing something wrong
- Limited access to acts of violence in the media (such as TV, internet, and video games)

When I healed (twenty years after getting out of my abusive relationship), I was determined to expose my young children to as many positive influences as possible to help set them on a path of developing healthy relationships. I also taught them to detect and understand the unhealthy messages we often see or hear in the media. This information is presented in detail in the second section of this book.

Chapter 6

"Why didn't you tell someone or leave?"
Reasons for Keeping Quiet and Staying

Over time, I pulled away from my family and friends. Initially, I did so because Brock made fun of them and put them down. Then, when he began abusing me, I didn't want to risk anyone seeing the way he talked and behaved toward me, so I pulled further away in order to hide it. I also ended up dropping out of many of the activities I'd been involved in, such as the Rotary Club and my church youth group.

In school, though, I remained a part of the student council, which provided what I considered a "safety net" during lunch. As part of the student council, I was required to work in the snack shop. While I had to talk to people to take their orders, the exchanges were always brief and involved nothing of a personal nature that might put me in jeopardy of getting into trouble with Brock. I found it was much safer to work the snack booth than to sit in the cafeteria with the opportunity to talk with various people during lunch.

I also worried about potential interactions with anyone I was likely to have outside of school. It was dangerous for me to spend much time with my friends because I might get into a situation Brock would disapprove of, such as talking to my best friend's boyfriend or another acquaintance. Although Brock and I had initially hung out with my friends, his displeasure with them increased until eventually there wasn't anything he liked about them. He relentlessly insisted they were a "bad influence" on me. Ultimately, I found it easier to break off many of my friendships than deal with the conflict and consequences those relationships created.

I'll never forget the day I ended my friendship with my best friend, Linda. Brock's harassment toward me when I hung out with her and his derogatory comments about her had continued to escalate for a few months, until one day I felt like my only choice was to end my friendship with her. I don't recall what he said that pushed me to this point, but I remember agonizing before calling and telling her, "You need to find a new ride to school." That was the last time we talked for a little over a year. (Thankfully, we mended our relationship, and for the past thirty years, she's been one of my closest friends.)

Despite fearing the trouble I could get into for it, I still wanted friends. So, when a girl from class invited me to go to a football game with her and her friends, I agreed. She didn't have a boyfriend, and we were just meeting up with a small group of her female friends. It felt like that would be a safe way to attend the game.

During the game, though, Brock approached me in the stands and asked me to walk with him for a minute. We left the group and made our way under the bleachers and away from others. He started asking me questions, interrogating me about who I was sitting with and who I had talked with. For the entire second quarter of the game, he proceeded to question and yell at me. It was clear he didn't like me being there, and I was ashamed of the way he was interrogating me. I desperately hoped my new friend couldn't hear the way he was berating me. Once I rejoined my new group of friends, I quickly made up an excuse and left early to avoid another confrontation with Brock. If I stayed, I knew I ran the risk of receiving further "discipline" from him later.

I eventually ended up making friends with a new group of girls that Brock had been friends with during junior high— therefore, he "approved" of these friendships. But since it was still safer for me to avoid social situations, I typically hung out with my new friends at one of our houses. I also continued to babysit a lot to occupy most of my free time and provide an excuse to stay away from social situations.

During my years with Brock, I slowly went from a person with a close group of friends and activities to a person with just one or two friends I held at a distance. I didn't do too much with them for fear of getting myself into a questionable situation. I also pulled away from my family by making excuses to retreat to my bedroom, consequently withdrawing from conversations and family activities. I became so distant from them emotionally that at times I felt like a stranger in my own house.

That summer I got a job at a frozen yogurt shop where I usually worked with a girl who attended another local high school. We developed a friendship I was grateful for. She and I were able to talk and hang out in a safe setting when business in the shop was slow. It was also easy to avoid attending any social activities with her since I was either at work, babysitting, or with my boyfriend.

But eventually the manager hired another teen, and the new coworker was a guy. This didn't sit well with Brock, who frequently asked about my schedule to find out when I would be working with the male coworker. When the other boy and I worked together, Brock would question me and accuse me of liking or flirting with him. But there wasn't an easy way to avoid working with him and the conflict it caused with Brock. As much as it would have helped, I knew it wasn't appropriate to ask my boss not to schedule me to work with the new boy. But, thankfully, I didn't have many shifts with my male coworker.

However, one night we had to close the store together. It normally took us about an hour to drain the yogurt machines, mop, and clean the store after closing. We talked while we cleaned up.

After we finished work, the two of us locked up the store and walked out into the parking lot. That's when I noticed Brock's car. Fear gripped me as questions raced through my mind: How long had he been there? What had he seen? Had I done anything inappropriate? Had I gotten too close physically to my coworker at any point?

There wasn't a way to avoid Brock, so, reluctantly, I walked over to his car and, with a knot in my stomach, got inside. He questioned me about the time I'd spent with my coworker. Then he informed me he'd been sitting outside watching us work together, looking for evidence of us behaving in a way he deemed unacceptable. Thankfully, he hadn't seen anything he felt was wrong. However, I was startled to learn that Brock had brought a baseball bat with him, intending to hurt the other guy if he acted "inappropriately" with me.

While Brock had hurt me physically before, the idea of his hurting someone else brought things to a whole new level. Bringing a baseball bat signified that Brock intentionally wanted to injure the other boy in a major way. While this realization alarmed me, at the time I didn't understand that his jealousy was completely out of control.

From that point forward, I was always careful when working with my male coworker. If something was needed out of the back, I made sure only one of us was back there at a time. After we closed the store to the public, I tried to do a job in another part of the store from him, such as putting up chairs and mopping while he put away the yogurt and toppings. Fortunately, at the end of the summer, the mom of a friend from school offered me a job at the daycare she directed. I quickly accepted, thinking, *How could Brock get upset with me for working with children?*

The job at the daycare also provided the solution to another problem. When Brock and I started dating, I was playing tennis on the school team. Tennis was during the last period, and practice usually continued after the end of the school day. So, while it kept me busy, it also created a problem: Brock was very jealous of the boys with whom I played tennis.

Worse, Brock's last-period class was shop class, and the doors to his class typically were left open. Since the classroom was located at the back of the school, near the tennis courts, sometimes Brock was able to keep an eye on me during class. Frequently, he saw something he disapproved of, and later he would give me a hard time about it, questioning me incessantly or accusing me of "bad" or flirtatious behavior.

For example, the tennis team usually had to run a lap around part of the school to warm up at the beginning of class. The last part of this lap took us right past the shop class. Now, I loved running, and I had a habit of sprinting at the end of the lap. One day, as I began sprinting, one of the boys I passed called out to me, and with a smile on my face, I threw him a comment back. This exchange was so insignificant I couldn't recall what was said, but since it occurred in front of the shop class, Brock later accused me of "flirting" with the other boy. As a result, I became a cautious runner, running slower and ensuring that there was always appropriate space between me and the boys on the team.

Since my job at the daycare started fifteen minutes after my last class ended, I had to quit the tennis team to get to work on time. The start time of my new job also didn't allow me much time to talk in the hallways after school, and this limited other opportunities for me to get into trouble with Brock. But I missed the interactions and laughter with other people. Through the course of our relationship, I became a lonely shell of a person.

At times, some of my high school friends suspected that my relationship with Brock wasn't healthy. The few times they tried to talk with me about it, out of shame, I quickly became defensive, lied, and pushed them away. They learned it was better not to bring it up.

One day Brock and I got into an argument outside as we were walking between classes, and the fight continued after the next class started. I was crying, and he was yelling at me so loudly that a teacher could hear us from her classroom inside the school. She came outside and told us we needed to return to class. I wanted so very badly for her to understand that what was happening between me and Brock was wrong. I wanted her to send me away from him and make it stop. But as much as I longed for the abuse to stop, I couldn't get the words out of my mouth to ask her—or anyone else—for help or to tell someone what was happening. (I found out later that the teacher suspected an abusive relationship and contacted my parents. They tried to intervene, but I grew defensive and pushed them away.)

On some level, I knew the abuse wasn't right, but it wasn't enough to make me leave. Instead, because of the shame I felt over it, I simply worked to hide it.

I honestly don't remember ever thinking about breaking up with Brock until the very end. Although abuse was prevalent in our relationship, it wasn't the only component, and there were other aspects to it that I enjoyed. For example, we frequently rented movies and went out for dinner. He walked me to class, and sometimes we would head off campus together for lunch. So, many parts of our relationship were just like any other dating relationship.

I can recall three times when other people reinforced that it was okay for me to stay with Brock, although of course they had no idea what was truly happening. The first was right after lunch one day at school. Brock and I had left the cafeteria and were outside, crossing through the courtyard to the building on the other side. In front of the building there were a few wide, brick pillars. I don't remember how it started, but Brock and I ended up playing a peekaboo game around one of the square pillars. We were smiling and laughing at each other, and the game ended with Brock wrapping me in a big bear hug and lifting me off the ground. In my next class, someone who had seen us playing approached me to tell me what "a cute couple" we were. Unfortunately, I used that remark to justify our relationship, telling myself if others thought we were a cute couple, then my relationship couldn't really be that bad.

Another time was during my senior year when people were voting for "best dressed," "most likely to succeed," and so forth. I was at a doctor appointment during the voting, and when I returned to school, as I passed people in the hall, some told me, "I voted for you!" When I told one of them I didn't know I'd been nominated for anything, they replied that Brock and I were one of the couples nominated to be "Best Couple." We didn't end up winning, but the nomination definitely created some confusing thoughts! On the one hand, I knew that just because we'd been together for a long time didn't make us a good couple. But it also made me wonder: If others thought we were a potential "Best Couple," was the relationship really as bad as I thought? Was I overreacting and being overly sensitive when it came to what Brock said and did?

The third was one afternoon when Brock and I went to his friend's house. It was just the three of us, and I knew better than to talk much with his friend. At some point, Brock and I moved to a room by ourselves, where he quickly became angry about something and started yelling at me. We were in there for quite a while as he berated me, and eventually I started crying. He didn't strike me, but he did hit the wall several times in anger. At one point his friend yelled, "C'mon, Brock!" in an effort to calm him down, but he never told Brock to stop, and he didn't come see what was going on.

Once Brock finally calmed down and we returned to the other room, I sat awkwardly in an armchair for a few minutes, my eyes puffy from crying. I was embarrassed about what his friend had overheard, but I also wondered why he hadn't stepped in more and interceded. I thought Brock's outburst was aggressive, and it humiliated me to be on the receiving end; but since his friend had just continued watching TV, it normalized the incident, and I wondered if it was really as big a deal as it felt to me.

What's Going On?

Statistics show that only 33 percent of abuse victims confide in another person about the abuse they're enduring, with the majority choosing to stay put in the relationship.[1] It may be difficult for those outside an abusive relationship who have never endured violence of any form to understand why so many don't leave such a relationship, but there are factors that influence abuse victims to stay.

For example, in an abusive relationship, it's common for the person being abused to bounce back and forth between abusive episodes and normal teen dating activities and feelings. So, despite experiencing ongoing abuse, many victims think about the times their partners are nice to them and end up deceiving themselves into thinking they have a normal dating relationship.

Here are just a few of the many reasons people can find it hard to leave an abusive relationship:[2]

- **The victim thinks the abuse is their fault.** The abuser often tells the victim they made them angry or did something to deserve the abuse. Even though no one deserves abuse, the victim believes the abuser.

- **The victim has low self-esteem, often as a result of the relationship.** The victim may believe they don't deserve any better and/or no one else will want to date them if they leave the relationship. Often, one of the elements of verbal abuse (see chapter 2) is for the abuser to name everything they think is wrong with their partner.

- **The victim holds false hopes.** Teenagers being abused often want to help their partner get better and may believe the violence will stop once they do. Teens may stay in an abusive relationship hoping that their abuser will change. They often only want the violence to stop, not for the relationship to end entirely.

- **The victim is experiencing shame.** It's hard for the victim to disclose that they've been abused. They also may feel shame over becoming involved with an abusive partner or for not leaving sooner. Additionally, they may worry that their friends and family will think badly of them once the truth is revealed.

- **The victim wants to be in a relationship.** Teens often feel pressure from their peers, family, or society to have a boyfriend or girlfriend.

- **Teens don't have much experience with dating relationships and may believe that jealousy is a sign of love.**

- **The teenage victim has a lack of information or resources available about dating abuse.** Many teens may never have heard of unhealthy relationships or dating abuse, and they may not recognize the warning signs.

- **Teens may be afraid the abuser will do something to hurt them or will hurt themselves if the abused person breaks up with them.**

I can honestly write today that all but the last reason in the above list fit my thoughts at different points during my relationship with Brock. While in the relationship, I focused on the good times and hoped Brock would change. I hoped the yelling and hitting would stop. Rather than consider leaving, I just accepted our relationship as it was. I also thought if I loved him enough, I could help him.

So, in the three years we dated, I never told anyone about what was truly happening. In our relationship, Brock had convinced me that the abuse was my fault. Deep down I knew his hitting and biting me was wrong, but I was too ashamed and embarrassed to tell someone about the way I was being treated or reach out for help.

What Can We Do?

Part two of this book includes detailed lists of warning signs that parents and other adults can become aware of and discuss with the adolescents in their lives. In particular, see chapters 13 and 14.

Unfortunately for me, Brock's control and abuse escalated as our relationship continued. The examples in the following chapters will illustrate the worst of the abuse I experienced as a teenager in my first relationship.

Chapter 7

"I'm going to kill you."
Physical Violence

The Ride

In the fall of my senior year, I needed a ride home from school one afternoon, and a girl in my homeroom class offered to drive me. Unfortunately, she was one of the few girls Brock had instructed me not to talk to, although I couldn't figure out why. I was nervous about accepting the ride, but since I didn't have any other options and didn't see Brock around, I thought it would be okay and took her up on her offer.

After school, she dropped me off at home. A little later Brock surprised me with a visit. When I answered the door, he explained he had come over because he "just wanted to see" me. He seemed laid back, even happy. Since I hadn't seen him when I'd gotten into my classmate's car earlier, I believed him and thought everything was fine. When he suggested we go for a drive, I accepted the invite. By then, I knew he didn't like being around my parents, so it was a good idea if I went somewhere else with him. I told my mom we were leaving, and the two of us headed out.

Brock drove us across the main street in town to a neighborhood where a new section was being developed; the roads were in place, but houses hadn't been built yet. Once we were there, Brock pulled up to a curb and stopped the car.

He turned to me and in a calm voice told me he had seen me get in the car with the girl he'd told me not to talk to. Because I hadn't listened, he was going to kill me.

He never said how he would kill me, but he had physically hurt me and instilled fear in me so many times before that I instinctively knew that if he wanted to kill me, he could. My mind frantically ran through ideas as to how to escape, but I realized even if I managed to get out of the car, he could quickly outrun and catch me. In shock and disbelief, I began to comprehend that while I was less than a mile from my house and less than half a mile from the part of the neighborhood where many families lived, the spot where we were parked was just remote enough that no one would hear me if I screamed for help. No one was going to be able to help me.

I began begging Brock not to hurt me and trying to reason with him while attempting to figure out how I could possibly get away from him. My words had no effect, as he relentlessly informed me how "easy" killing me would be. As if he could read my mind, he callously said, "No one will hear you scream, and it will take a long time for your body to be found."

I fell apart, crying hysterically. This only made Brock angrier. (He always got angrier when I cried.) I don't remember why, but eventually, he stopped the threats and began to comfort me.

We talked for a while, and it became clear to me that I needed to listen to him going forward. (Years later, I found out Brock had been dating the other girl at the same time he was dating me. He had told me not to talk to her because he didn't want us to figure out he was seeing both of us.)

Although Brock didn't physically hurt me that day, I knew from that point on that being killed by him was a possibility. And still I continued to date him, doing my best to be a "good girlfriend" and focus on the good times as much as possible while hoping he would change, that his yelling and hitting would stop. Rather than consider leaving, again I just accepted this as part of our relationship.

As I've mentioned previously, despite the ongoing abuse, I always hoped each time would be the last. When my boyfriend was nice, it was easy to deceive myself into thinking I had a normal dating relationship.

The Rodeo

In the spring of my senior year, Brock and I had tickets to the rodeo with his parents. A few days before the rodeo, Brock told me not to wear my overalls when we went. I knew he found me attractive in my overalls (trendy back in 1988!), and, being a typical teen, I wanted to wear something I knew my boyfriend liked on me. I couldn't imagine why he had asked me not to wear something he usually liked on me, so I naïvely ignored his instructions and wore the overalls.

After getting ready for the date, I drove over to his house. I was nervous when I arrived, wondering how he would react at the sight of me in the overalls. But he didn't say anything, so I assumed everything was all right. His parents had already left for the rodeo grounds, so the two of us went in his car to meet up with them.

Once there, we held hands, talked, and enjoyed watching the rodeo and performance together. The entire time, I was careful to control where I looked in the arena, never scanning the crowd in case he thought I might be looking at another boy.

When the performance was over, Brock suggested we go back to his house while his parents stayed to walk around the grounds some more. I agreed, and when we arrived at his house, we sat on the couch together. As he moved over close to me, he quietly and coldly told me my first mistake was wearing the overalls, and my second mistake was coming home with him.

Instinctively, I knew this time something was different from the many other times Brock had been angry with me. It was clear he was outraged and I needed to get away from him—not just out of his immediate reach, but *out of the house.* In fact, I didn't think even getting outside in the front yard where people could see us would be enough to deter him; no, I wanted to get in my car and drive away. Far, far away from Brock, his hands, and his anger.

My mind was racing in a panic. We were still sitting close together on the couch. Besides getting out of my seat, the other problem was that before leaving for the rodeo I had left my car keys in his bedroom at the back of the house. I was going to have to jump away from him, run through the house to grab my keys, and then dash back through the house and out into the front yard to get into my car. The house was small, so I thought maybe I could accomplish this. I believed it was my only chance to escape Brock's rage.

Somehow, I did manage to bolt away from him on the couch and make it to my keys. But as I came out of the bedroom and stepped into the hallway, he met me—with a rifle. I fell apart, sobbing with my car keys in my hand, but my back pressed hard against the hallway wall.

As Brock stood inches from me with the gun in his hand, I slid down the wall to the floor, my entire body trembling. I was terrified. I wanted to get away but didn't know how. All I could do was sit and cry. Terrified and defeated, I knew I was about to die.

Brock let me sob for a few minutes before he told me to stand up. With the rifle still in his hand, he led me back to the family room to sit on the couch. Instead of shooting me, he started to talk to me.

He told me he was angry and he wanted me to understand what I had done wrong. But he also said he loved me and didn't want to lose me. In his eyes, if he found me attractive in those overalls, then other boys would also. He didn't want me to wear them in front of other boys, and I wasn't to wear them outside of school. He even told me he was acting this way for my own good, and that he wanted to protect our relationship because he cared for me so much.

What's Going On?

There haven't been many studies on homicide rates in teen dating violence, but one of the larger studies was conducted in 2018. For the study, researchers analyzed homicides of eleven- to eighteen-year-olds across thirty-two states.[1] The study found that 7 percent of the victims were killed by a current (62.7 percent) or former dating partner. Ninety percent of these victims were girls of an average age of 16.8. The rate of homicides in nineteen- to twenty-four-year-olds perpetrated by an intimate partner rose to 15 percent.

The study went on to report the following:

The methods used most often to kill a dating partner:
- A firearm (most often a handgun): 61 percent
- A blunt object: 25 percent
- Strangulation or hanging: 7.5 percent

The murders occurred in these locations:
- The victim's home: 38 percent
- Someone else's home or apartment: 36 percent
- On the street or sidewalk, or in an alley: 7 percent
- In a motor vehicle or parking lot/garage: 6 percent

Below are the reasons given for the person to murder their romantic interest:
- Twenty-seven percent cited a breakup, a desired (but unfulfilled) relationship, or jealousy. In other words, the victim ended or would not begin a relationship with the perpetrator, or the perpetrator was jealous.
- Twenty-five percent were caused by some kind of altercation (e.g., the pair was arguing, and the fighting escalated).

- Eight percent were the result of reckless behavior with a firearm.
- Seven percent said an unwanted pregnancy led them to commit the crime. (The murder was a way to terminate the pregnancy.)

What Can We Do?

When our kids are young, we're consistent in teaching them things like how to avoid talking to strangers, how to safely cross the street, how to be careful around a hot stove, and how to manage any number of other situations that can be harmful. In other words, we communicate information on situations and things that can be harmful so our children can stay safe. As our kids get older, we need to continue offering similar messages regarding situations they might encounter and safety measures they may need to use.

Parents, teachers, youth directors, neighbors, and any adult who has the opportunity to speak into the life of a child or youth can remind them

- always to trust their gut instinct;
- to go places only with people they trust;
- that if they ever feel uncomfortable, it's okay to say no to an invitation;

- that if they get into a situation in which they're not comfortable, they should leave it as quickly as possible; and
- that if they ever need help, they should call or confide in a trusted adult.

Additionally, we need to be aware of the protective rules that exist on school campuses and in cities or towns. For instance, if a tween or teen confides in us about the abuse, we can help them seek protection at their school and also get them a civil protection order. If safety measures don't exist or don't provide adequate protection in a community, we should begin advocating for stronger protection and better laws. Doing this can make a big difference in protecting all youth in those communities.

Chapter 8

"Does anyone care?"

Despair and Depression

It felt like everything I did was wrong. With Brock I got in trouble for saying the wrong thing, dressing the wrong way, or acting the wrong way. As a result, I no longer believed in myself or considered myself worthy of being loved. Even after spending time together on a "good" date with Brock, I still wondered if he really cared about me. I wanted to feel his love emotionally—to know that he cared about me.

A few months after I started dating Brock, my parents began guessing that my relationship with him wasn't healthy and tried to question me about it. But because of the shame I already carried, when they tried to reach out, I quickly became defensive. Although they loved me and were worried about me, their questions felt confrontational, and I pushed them away even as the abuse grew—often running straight to Brock. When asking me questions or expressing concern didn't work, my parents tried to limit the time I spent with Brock. Often it felt like I was in trouble for dating him.

Before dating Brock, I had been in trouble for some low grades, and during my relationship with him, my grades didn't improve. So, academics also still tended to be an issue between my parents and me. As my relationship with Brock progressed, my relationship with my parents filled with more and more tension. I occasionally still went sailing with them, but I was usually sullen on the boat, escaping to the bow to "do homework" or take a nap.

It felt as if I couldn't do anything right, and someone was always upset with me. I wondered why I couldn't be loved just for who I was. I began experiencing an overwhelming sense of sadness and frequently cried when I was alone in my car.

In bed at night, I often cried myself to sleep, wondering if anybody loved me. Despite having people around me who said they cared about me, I felt utterly alone. I didn't understand these feelings.

Despair. Barely functioning. Getting by. Looking back, that's how I would describe my life when I was dating Brock.

I was too enmeshed in the abuse to see clearly, and I didn't realize it was the abuse causing these negative feelings. I couldn't put a label on it then, but now I know I suffered from depression caused by the abuse, fear, isolation, and shame.

I began to think about hurting myself—not because I wanted to be hurt, but because I thought if something terrible happened to me, I could see if anyone really cared about me. While driving my car alone, I frequently thought about crashing into something like a tree or a concrete barrier. I wanted to injure myself enough to be hospitalized just to see if anyone would come to visit me. Then I would know they cared. And I hoped if they saw me seriously hurt or injured, they would realize what I meant to them.

While driving, I would try to calculate how I could veer off the road and cause enough damage to injure myself and be hospitalized, but not enough harm to kill myself or cause serious injury. I thought about what would happen if I struck something with the passenger side of the car. Would it be enough to injure me and put me in the hospital, but not quite enough to cause me really serious injury? Or did I need to strike the front of the car? Or even impact the driver's side, to increase the likelihood that I would be injured? I didn't want to just have an accident and have someone get mad at me for messing up yet again. I needed to be injured just enough that they would overlook the damage and instead demonstrate their care and concern for me.

But I didn't know what would actually happen if I struck something. I didn't know if the accident would be enough to injure me without causing lasting harm. So, while I continued to have these thoughts, I never acted on them.

My salvation during this time was God. Thankfully, I knew God not only loves each of us but loves us un- conditionally—including me—and I frequently turned to Him. I would cry out to God, asking why others couldn't love me the same way He did. I was so grateful God loved me.

Knowing God loves me unconditionally is what saved me during this part of my life and gave me hope. Despite pulling away from my church youth group and avoiding church, there were many times I clung to God. I cried out and prayed to Him when I felt alone.

> *For I am the* Lord *your God who takes hold of your right hand and says to you, Do not fear; I will help you.*
>
> (Isaiah 41:13)

> *And surely I am with you always, to the very end of the age.*
>
> (Matthew 28:20)

God was my strength. He was my safe haven. Without God's love, I don't know what would have happened to me then or where I'd be today.

What's Going On?

The confidence of a teen in an abusive relationship is chipped away gradually by their abuser. Steadily over time, the abuser demolishes the victim's self-esteem. The victim doesn't recognize this, and they end up feeling defeated and demoralized. They don't believe in themselves, and they doubt their own worth. They feel like they can't do much right in the eyes of their partner and possibly others. They're isolated and alone without anyone to confide in, let alone to do something fun, relax, or laugh with.

Teens in an abusive dating relationship

- are more likely to be depressed or anxious,
- may experience post-traumatic stress disorder as a result of the abuse, and
- may have suicidal thoughts or attempt suicide due to the psychological impact of the abuse.[1]

What Can We Do?

Adults should know the warning signs of depression and suicidal thoughts so they can discern whether the youth in their lives are displaying and suffering from any of the following:[2]

Warning Signs of Depression:
- Lack of interest in activities they used to enjoy
- Lack of energy

- Changes in appetite or body weight—either lack of appetite/eating or gaining weight
- Changes in sleeping habits—has trouble getting to sleep or staying asleep, or oversleeps
- Negative self-talk or putting themselves down
- Irritability or easily becoming angry
- Headaches, stomachaches, or other unexplained aches and pains
- Trouble concentrating or lower grades (due to inability to focus)
- Feeling hopeless (only the teen may notice this)

Warning Signs of Suicidal Thoughts and/or Attempts:
- Making comments such as "Everyone would be better off without me."
- Making comments about harming or killing themselves
- Becoming preoccupied with death or dying
- Giving away items that have always meant a lot to them or that they wouldn't share with others in the past
- Demeanor suddenly changing from being down for a significant amount of time to being happy

If you observe any of the warning signs above, contact a counselor or suicide hotline for advice. (See the resources at the end of the book.) Try mentioning to the teen that they don't seem as happy as they once were and gently suggest they see a counselor.

If you are a parent, a grandparent, a neighbor, or someone who works with youth, say something kind to the tweens and teens you come in contact with to show them you care. Your kind word may be the only one they hear that day.

Parents can remind their kids often that **they are loved for who they are—by their family, by their friends, and by God**. Because of the abuse victim's defensive nature or the feelings of defeat the youth may be experiencing, it may not seem like they're listening or that your words are making a difference—but they are. Continue to keep trying to share these messages with them.

Chapter 9

"Look what you made me do."
Sexual Assault

For my birthday during my senior year, I planned to go to the beach and hang out for the afternoon with two friends. One of the girls was a cautious and reserved friend from junior high, so Brock thought it was okay if I occasionally spent time with her. The other was my friend from the yogurt shop.

Since my birthday is in early April, it was after spring break and before any summer crowds. I concluded it was a safe time for me to go since it would be a relatively quiet time at the beach. My friends were conservative, and they weren't guy crazy. None of us drank. As a result of such careful planning in terms of the friends I was going with and the timing of the trip, I thought Brock would be okay with it.

I couldn't have been more wrong, which I found out a few days before the trip, when Brock and I headed to my house during our school lunch break. My parents were at work, and as we walked into the house, he started kissing me and leading me back to my bedroom. When we got to my room, he leaned me back toward the bed as he pulled up my skirt.

Suddenly he started punching my legs from both sides. The pain was intense, and I ineffectively tried to cover myself. Just as swiftly as it started, his attack was over.

Even though Brock hitting me was a regular occurrence, every time still came as a surprise and shock to me. We were kissing and being affectionate, so how could I have done something he considered wrong?

Brock explained he was jealous and didn't want anyone at the beach to find me attractive, so he wanted to "blemish" me to ensure I was unattractive to other boys who might be at the beach. He didn't want anyone else to want me.

When my friends and I went to the beach a few days later, I ended up wearing a long shirt for most of the day. It wasn't quite long enough to cover the bruises, and when my friends asked about it, I explained that I'd been energetically lifting weights in the garage. I told them I hadn't realized I'd gotten so carried away—so much that I'd let the weights hit my legs pretty hard when I lowered them each time.

I don't think my friends believed me, but they didn't push it. By this point in my relationship with Brock, I think they realized asking me personal questions only made me run away from them.

Graduation

High school graduation was a lonely time. Brock wouldn't allow me to go to any of the parties and celebrations. When our graduating class had a pool party at the local country club, I couldn't go because Brock didn't want me in a bathing suit in front of others.

On graduation night, Brock told me not to go to any of the parties. But the rule didn't apply to him. He planned to go to one of the parties and allowed me to go to dinner with my friend from the yogurt shop. Our plan was that I would pick him up at 10:00 p.m. from the party and spend the night with him at his house. I told my parents I was spending the night at my friend's house.

After we graduated, Brock went on to the party while my friend and I went to dinner as planned. We finished dinner earlier than I'd expected, so she wanted to try to find a party. This was a problem since I wasn't allowed to go to any parties, not even the one Brock was at. I couldn't tell my friend this, of course, so at first we drove to the party where Brock was. But when we reached the house, I made an excuse about why I didn't want to go in and drove my friend home early. Not knowing where else to go, I went to Brock's house to wait for the time I was to pick him up.

I didn't know what Brock's parents knew of the plan, so when they answered the door, I just said I was there to wait until it was time to pick up Brock from a party. They let me in, and I sat and watched TV with them.

I was embarrassed to have to sit there with his parents. I didn't like missing all the graduation celebrations and being excluded from Brock's plans; it made me feel like a loser. When it was almost 10:00, I drove the mile or so from his house to the party. I knew better than to go inside, so I parked out front and waited for him.

After several minutes, I saw Brock running across the front yard of the house toward my car. He was running in a funny way, and I laughed, thinking he was intentionally being goofy. But when Brock got in the car, he immediately started pummeling my face. All I felt was pain, terrible pain. I was terrified and began sobbing. Finally, Brock started using words instead of his fists.

He started questioning me, and slowly I realized he was drunk and thought I had arrived several hours late. Someone at the party had told him it was 1:00 a.m. instead of 10:00 p.m., and he thought because I'd picked him up "late," I'd been out with someone else. He wanted to know where I'd been, why I was late, and whom I'd been with. As I tearfully explained, Brock finally started to believe I was on time. He settled down and told me to drive him home.

Although Brock had calmed down, I was still terrified, and this time I wanted help. On the way to the party, I had passed the flashing lights of a police car; the officers had pulled someone over. They were about two blocks away, and I would pass them again on my way to Brock's house. Over and over in my mind, I thought about how I might be able to get out of the car and run to those officers. As my mind raced through how to get out of the car, I realized—over and over again—that Brock, who was sitting right beside me, would be able to grab me before I could stop the car and open the door.

As I turned the corner to the street where the police were, Brock saw them too. In a stern tone, he told me to drive carefully and not let the officers see anything suspicious. Too scared to try to make it out of the car to the safety of the police, I drove right past the officers, past those who could have helped me. A few minutes later we pulled up at his house.

As Brock walked toward the front door, I trailed a few steps behind. I did not want to go into that house. I did not want to go into that house *with him,* and I did not want his parents to see what their son had done to me. I wanted to get in my car and go away, but I didn't know where to go.

His mom opened the front door and was shocked at seeing my face swollen and bloody. I went inside, where she gave me some ice to ease the pain and swelling. Brock bounced between anger and remorse. He was furious and yelled at his parents; then he would see my face and cry over what he had done to me.

For the next several hours, Brock alternated between being enraged at his family and being remorseful whenever he looked at me. His parents kept trying to convince him to lie down and go to sleep, and finally, he agreed—but only if I would lie down next to him. I didn't want to, but I was afraid if he saw my reluctance, he would blow up again. I lay down next to him, he draped his arm across me, and within minutes he passed out.

I wanted to be anywhere but there. But I was afraid if I moved or tried to leave the bed, I risked waking him up. Eventually I attempted moving, and when he stayed asleep, I went into the family room with his parents until they went to bed. Then I half-slept in an armchair until morning, when I quietly let myself out of the house.

When I arrived home that morning, my parents were extremely concerned when they saw me. I had a black eye, and I'm pretty sure a broken nose (I never went to the doctor to find out for sure). I told them that there was a girl at school who looked similar to me, and sometimes people got us confused; I said that last night someone had been angry with her and when they saw me from behind, they'd mistaken me for the other girl and punched me before realizing their mistake.

They didn't believe me; but by then they had learned if they pushed me, I would only back further away from them. So they let it drop.

I was supposed to work at the daycare that day, and when I tried to call in sick, my boss responded that I needed to come to work. It was one of the best things that ever happened to me. You see, I didn't fake being sick when I called in, but I did tell her the fake story about how I got punched. Even though I explained I was worried that the bruises on my face would frighten the two-year-olds I was responsible for, my boss told me they'd be fine, and I needed to come in.

Do you know what? The kids were wonderful! Full of innocence and unconditional love, not one of them asked what had happened. They all treated me normally, which I needed so much. During the afternoon, the group of kids and I sat on the carpet so I could read them a story. As we sat down, one of them noticed my face. Instead of asking any questions, she simply looked at me, said I had a boo-boo, and leaned over to kiss it better. I had to hold back tears as this child's kindness and compassion consoled me.

The other good thing that came from going to work that day was the parents of my group of toddlers. As each arrived to pick up their child, they of course asked what had happened. While I stuck with the fake story, having to face so many people forced me, just a little, to admit to myself what was really going on.

Once at College

You might think that I wouldn't end up going away to college because of the extremely possessive and jealous relationship I was in, but amazingly I did. I picked a college that was two hours away, and Brock didn't oppose it. If he had objected, I'm sure I wouldn't have gone.

My freshman year, I came home almost every weekend as soon as my Friday classes ended. Shortly after the start of school, I got a new job at the mall in my hometown and worked there every weekend while attending school the rest of the week. While at college, though, I was careful to make friends with only a handful of girls, because even with a distance of two hours from Brock, I had learned to act carefully and follow his rules.

I came home the weekend of my nineteenth birthday, which marked the beginning of a turning point.

Since Brock didn't want to celebrate my birthday with my family, he planned to pick me up after I'd had dinner and cake with my family and neighbors. He didn't even want to come inside and greet my family and friends, so I needed to "be ready and come outside" when he pulled up. Meeting him outside like this had been standard practice for quite a while.

Dinner and cake ran later than expected, so when Brock arrived outside, we were still in the middle of eating cake and ice cream. When I didn't come out right away, he came to the door and joined us inside while we finished eating. He was acting pleasant and nice, but still I hurried to finish so as not to upset him.

When I finished eating, he and I headed out. He was fine in the car, and I relaxed a little. He took me to a local park, where we walked around while holding hands. At one point, Brock started to tell me about a book on housebuilding he'd checked out of the library and how he wanted to build a house for the two of us someday. While it was a relief that he wasn't upset with me, I was startled to hear these thoughts.

I hadn't ever imagined what a future with Brock would look like, and despite my commitment to be with only one man, the thought now of spending the rest of my life with Brock gave me an odd feeling in the pit of my stomach.

Yet I also didn't see our relationship ending. Rather than consider and analyze my feelings, however, I just moved on, so relaxed and thankful he wasn't upset with me.

After a time, we got in the car and headed home. On the way, Brock pulled off the highway and drove down a dirt road. He parked in a quiet and dark spot, and we started to fool around in the car.

As we kissed, he rolled on top of me in the passenger seat and pulled down my shorts. Suddenly he placed his arm across my chest to hold me down and quicky reached his other hand behind him into the glove box and pulled out a flashlight. Before I knew what was going on, he began shoving it inside me, over and over again, all the while asking if this was "how big the guy was back at college." (The entire time I dated Brock, I never dated anyone else or did anything with another boy.)

I couldn't move and I couldn't push him off me. When he decided it was over, he silently climbed off me and started to drive the rest of the way home. I was scared, humiliated, and in shock. All I remember about the rest of the drive home is feeling broken—completely broken.

In the days after, I tried not to think about what Brock had done. But when the memory popped up in my mind, I thought of what he had done as rape, then quickly told myself it didn't count. This was someone I was intimate with, so what he'd done to me couldn't be rape. Besides, Brock had used an object; he hadn't forced himself on me. So, I rationalized, it couldn't be considered rape.

Years later, a counselor told me that what I'd endured was a violent form of rape because Brock had used an object on me. It took me twenty years to admit and believe I had been raped.

What's Going On?

The Susan B. Anthony Project, an organization that provides support to victims of domestic violence and sexual assault, states that "just like any sexual assault, date or acquaintance rape is not about love, passion, or even sex. **It's about aggression and violence**."[1] In date rape, the assault is committed by someone the victim knows, usually someone they're dating or a social acquaintance. The victim does not consent to the sexual activity or is unable to say no (for example, when alcohol or a date rape drug is used).

According to the California Coalition Against Sexual Assault's *2008 Report: Research on Rape and Violence*, a study of 1,600 juvenile sexual assault offenders nationwide revealed:[2]

- "Only 33% of the juveniles perceived sex as a way to demonstrate love or caring for another person"
- "23.5% perceived sex as a way to feel a sense of power and control"
- "9.4% perceived sex as a way to dissipate any anger they might be feeling at the time"
- "8.4% percent perceived sex as a means with which they could punish another person."

The 2015 Youth Risk Behavior survey found that, among dating teens, "10.6% of students had been forced to do sexual things (counting being kissed, touched, or physically forced to have sexual intercourse) they did not want to do by someone they were dating or going out with one or more times during the 12 months before the survey."[3]

The Susan B. Anthony Project shares these common reasons victims don't report rape:[4]

- They are worried others won't believe them.
- They're concerned that others, including the perpetrator, will be angry with them. (In many cases there have been reports of friends, peers, or the community being angry with the victim for accusing the perpetrator.)
- They blame themselves or think they did something that led to it (such as going somewhere isolated with the perpetrator, dressing too provocatively, or drinking too much).
- They're not sure what happened to them was really rape. (They know or are dating the perpetrator, and/or they didn't say no because they worried about repercussions.)

The Project also shares some common myths about sexual assault:[5]

- "Guys don't get raped."
- "Guys can't stop once they start having sex."
- "They're dating. That's not rape."
- "He's the nicest guy ever! Not a rapist!"
- "He/She lies about everything."
- "They've had sex a million times already."

A victim of date rape, or any sexual assault, is never at fault. No one has the right to force or coerce another person into having sex.

What Can We Do?

Parents can help educate and support their kids to take the following actions to protect themselves:

- Do their best to stay safe by not going somewhere they're not comfortable (for example, to a secluded spot or an unchaperoned party).
- Choose group dates or public settings as date spots instead of spending time alone with the person they're dating.
- Set boundaries (for instance, on things like where they want to draw the line on sexual activity).
- Understand that any kind of pressure is not okay (see chapter 3 for examples).
- Know it's okay to say no, and that they have the right to say no.
- Understand that sexual abuse can occur even if both partners have previously consented to sex with one another.

- Trust their instincts—if something doesn't feel right to them, it's most likely not, and it's okay to leave that situation or say they're not going to go someplace.
- Stay sober or be careful not to drink very much so they are able to take care of themselves. If they choose to drink, they should be cautious about drinking in public or around people they don't know well, as their drink may get spiked or contain a date rape drug.
- Call a hotline or the police if they don't have an adult they feel comfortable confiding in.

Talking about this information may be uncomfortable for parents, your tween/teen, or both. But the more information we provide our kids, the better equipped they will be to recognize potentially harmful situations and keep themselves safe.

Chapter 10

"Breaking up is hard to do."

Breakup Risks and Dangers

A few weeks after my nineteenth birthday, Brock and I were talking on the phone while I was at college. Somehow the night of my birthday came up, and Brock said something that made me realize his attack on me with the flashlight had been planned. He explained that he'd punished me because I hadn't been ready and hadn't come out to his car when he'd arrived. The way he described this, it made me understand that, to him, the episode was a punishment I deserved.

Punishment? Deserved? Because of what Brock expressed during the rest of our conversation, I grasped for the first time that what he had done to me that night had been premeditated. Planned. On purpose. To inflict punishment.

Previously I had always believed his attacks were a snap or knee-jerk reaction—something he couldn't control. But as I reflected on the conversation, I began to comprehend that *this* attack had been planned. Like a single drop of water on a still lake creating a ripple effect, something began to change in me.

I didn't realize it at the time, but over the next several weeks, I began to gradually pull away from him and wonder if this was the relationship I wanted. When I returned home at the end of the school year, for the first time since we'd started dating, occasionally I chose not to spend time with Brock. In July, I finally found the courage to break up with him.

> Please note that, although I'm going to share with you how I broke up with Brock, **I would never recommend this approach**. I deliberately put myself in a very vulnerable position, not realizing what a foolish risk I was taking with my life. **I was NOT safe in the way I broke up with Brock.** At the time, I wasn't aware of any of the information I'll share with you later in this chapter and book.

One July evening I told my parents I was going to Brock's for a bit, then to my friend Linda's to spend the night. (I can't remember if I told either my parents or Linda that I was planning to break up with Brock.) I drove to Brock's house, and after I arrived, we went into his bedroom.

This night I felt empowered. The decision to break up with him, to end the relationship, had given me a strength I'd never had during the relationship. I didn't think of all the times he had threatened to kill me or about the gun he had in his house. While I don't remember what I said to him, I do remember that, for once, I felt confident facing him.

I boldly stood up to him as I ended things. I actually wanted to provoke him to hit me, so I could go to the police and press charges for all the times I hadn't done so in the past.

I'm thankful now that he didn't raise a hand—or do anything worse—to me that night. Instead, our conversation lasted about an hour, and then I left. I drove straight to Linda's house, called my parents to let them know I was there, and then, for the first time, told Linda some of the details of my relationship with Brock.

Breakup Danger

The breakup and the time after the breakup are the most dangerous time periods in an abusive relationship. The person who wants to control the other person has lost control, and their aggression escalates to gain the control back. When we hear stories in the news about someone killing an ex-girlfriend, boyfriend, or spouse, it's usually when the victim is trying to leave the abuser. In fact, 75 percent of homicides related to domestic violence occurred when the victims tried to leave their relationship. **In the two years after the breakup, there is also a 75 percent increase in the risk of violence.**[1]

Although Brock didn't get aggressive with me when I told him we were over, he still pursued me after I ended the relationship, calling me every few weeks. And when an acquaintance told him I had started to date someone new, Brock called me and threatened to mail my new boyfriend suggestive pictures Brock had taken of me while we were dating. (This was before cell phones.)

Brock had taken the photos before we'd become intimate, after I agreed to his suggestion that he take them as an alternative to my having sex with him. At the time, he had told me he thought I was attractive, and if I wouldn't have sex with him, couldn't I at least let him take a "sexy" picture of me? I had reluctantly agreed, and so Brock had asked me to remove my shirt and put on a hunting jacket over my bra, then remove my jeans as well and sit seductively on his bed.

I hadn't been comfortable wearing the jacket that way or posing for the pictures, but I did want to put off having sex, so I had gone along with it. But now I was scared. I didn't want my new boyfriend to think I was a bad person for agreeing to sexy photos that showed me wearing what looked like a jacket with nothing underneath. And I definitely didn't want others to see what I'd done. But I didn't give in to Brock's demands that I break things off with the new guy, and thankfully Brock didn't follow through on his threat to mail my new boyfriend the pictures.

When I moved back to school that fall, Brock didn't call me as often. Rather than feeling relieved and thinking he was finally moving on, I was afraid he would do something worse, like show up at my college. I was on edge, always feeling like I needed to look over my shoulder and make sure he wasn't nearby. Out of fear for what could happen and wanting to prepare my roommates, I confessed to them that my previous boyfriend had hit me. (Notice the use of the word *confess*? That's what my past relationship always felt like—something I had done wrong that I needed to confess to others.) I didn't provide many details, and although they were surprised, they were also supportive.

Brock never did show up, but several months later, when I was at my parents' house one weekend, he called me. He wanted to see me and threatened to kill himself if I didn't see him. As I listened to him speak, I could tell he was drunk. I had no idea whether the threats were true, so I stayed on the phone with him. Many times I tried to end the call, but he kept threatening to kill himself unless I agreed to meet with him.

After a few hours of this, I finally promised I would meet up with him in two days in an effort to calm him down and in the hope that he wouldn't kill himself. Before Brock hung up, he made me promise over and over that I was really going to meet up with him.

I had no intention of actually meeting him, but I did want someone to keep an eye on him in case the threats had been real. So, the next day I called his parents to let them know I would not be meeting Brock the following day and to alert them to the dangers of what he had said. At this point they thanked me for talking to him the day before, explaining that just before he called me, he had been threatening to kill himself and they'd just gotten a rifle away from him.

I wish I could say that was the end of my contact with Brock. It wasn't. But fortunately, nothing serious ever happened from that point forward, and eventually, Brock did call me less and less. But after I joined Facebook, he sent me two separate messages. I never responded, and I blocked all contacts I could find with his name. It was very alarming that twenty years after our breakup, Brock was still thinking about me.

What's Going On?

The period after the breakup is particularly risky for the person who has been abused, **not only because of the elevated harm the ex-partner might inflict but also because the**

survivor has been isolated. The survivor needs to heal from the shame, guilt, and low self-esteem the abusive relationship has caused. They need a "safety net," or they're likely to return to the relationship. But since the survivor has usually been isolated from other relationships, they are lonely when the relationship ends and often miss their dating partner. **Unless they have some sort of safety net, the survivor is likely to return to their abusive ex-partner.** (Safety nets include reconnecting with healthy friendships, getting involved in school and/or church activities, and reestablishing relationships with their family. More will be covered in the next chapter.)

I believe getting out of an abusive relationship is probably very similar to the new skills an alcoholic or drug user needs to learn to stay sober or clean. Just as the shame and guilt from previous actions can make it hard for an alcoholic or drug abuser to form new relationships, the layers of shame and guilt from an abusive relationship also make it difficult to reach out and form new relationships. And just as a drug abuser or alcoholic often returns to old habits, the victim often returns to the abuser out of habit. In fact, *some victims leave the relationship as many as seven or eight times before they're finally able to break free for good*.[2]

What Can We Do?

We need to provide gentle support. I specify "gentle" because the survivor is processing a *lot*.

They may be grieving the relationship. Even though they're ready to be out of the abuse, there are aspects of their ex-partner they may still care about. It's likely their partner was a big part of their life and consumed much of their time, so they may miss them or feel lonely.

They may feel exposed. Even if they've shared only a few of the details of the relationship, or maybe none at all, they may still wonder what others know and what others may think of them for having been in that relationship.

We should make sure we're available if they want to talk. If and when they are ready to talk, be prepared to listen and to hold back on asking many questions. Just let them talk about what's on their minds and whatever they want to bring up.

Support the survivor in getting involved in activities, but be careful not to push them. They may have been told what to do by their abuser, and being pushed may be a trigger for them.

Most of all, just be available, offer kind words or support, and give them space as needed.

Chapter 11

"I just want to be normal."
Trying to Move On

Almost a year after breaking up with Brock, I met Art through one of my roommates, and we began dating. He was a senior and had played football his first few years in college. He was similar in stature to Brock, but Art was kind and thoughtful.

A few weeks after this new relationship began, my roommate asked me to drive her to buy a six-pack of beer. Afterward, she and I ended up stopping at a party on our way home, where one of Art's friends started hitting on me. I became uncomfortable and asked my roommate if we could leave. She said yes, and we did before things became more awkward.

The next day I was nervous all day, knowing I had to tell Art what had happened the night before and worrying about his reaction. Because I had always been in trouble with Brock, I worried that being hit on by Art's friend was somehow my fault.

Art arrived to pick me up for our date that night, and a few minutes after we got into his car, I told him about the party the night before. He asked me if his friend had been there, and I said yes. Then he asked if his friend had hit on me. Once again, I said yes—and that was it. The end of the conversation about it.

Art wasn't mad.

Art didn't think it was my fault.

Art didn't yell at me.

Art didn't break up with me.

Art didn't hit me.

The fact that Art didn't blame me and that he did absolutely nothing to me as a result of what had happened the night before was completely foreign to me. So, as much as I didn't want an abusive relationship, I now also didn't know or understand what a normal relationship was like.

What's Going On?

Moving on from an abusive relationship without fear or shame is difficult for many victims of abuse. Over the course of twenty years, I disclosed the abuse in my high school relationship to only a few friends. As for the handful of times I started seriously dating someone, I thought of my high school relationship as a dark secret I had to "admit" to my new partner. This was because I continued to perceive the abuse in the relationship as my fault and therefore something I should be ashamed of.

Often, when I confided in a friend or new boyfriend, I received the same response. They were shocked and usually said something along the lines of "I can't believe you'd put up with that." Since my friends typically describe me as strong, I'm sure it was hard for them to comprehend that I could have been victimized in this way.

But the sad reality is that whenever someone responded to my story with disbelief, it only reinforced the shame I carried. However, over time I realized they didn't understand abusive relationships, and they didn't mean to unwittingly make me feel bad or unsupported.

Shame isn't the only thing survivors are at risk of experiencing. Once the survivor is fortunate enough to break free, they're in jeopardy of getting involved in other risky behaviors. Studies show that five years after the relationship ends, teens who were victims of an abusive dating relationship are more likely to engage in smoking and/or heavy or binge drinking, experience depression and/or thoughts of suicide, or end up in another abusive relationship.[1]

And if the survivor is fortunate enough not to return to the old abusive relationship or get involved in a new one, they need to relearn the components of and what to expect in healthy relationships (see chapter 2).

I'd like to write that the road to normal after a breakup, especially a breakup of an abusive relationship, is an easy one. But the truth is it's not.

When everyone else was figuring out who they were and what was important to them during their high school and college years, I had been so severely restricted and controlled that I was essentially a prisoner or hostage. For three long years, someone had told me whom I could talk to, how I could dress, how I could act, and what activities I could and couldn't do. Once I was away at college and on my own, I ended up making several mistakes on my road back to healthy relationships. I hope I can help others avoid these same mistakes.

What Can We Do?

For parents, teachers, other adults, and friends who want to help survivors of an abusive relationship, here are some key actions to **help survivors of abuse heal and form healthy relationships after a breakup**.

1. **Encourage them to seek a counselor or therapist knowledgeable in abuse recovery and/or attend a support group.** Victims form many unhealthy habits and

perceptions during an abusive relationship. It's important for survivors to heal and learn about the components of healthy relationships, or else the survivor risks getting involved with another harmful or abusive person.

- While most of my subsequent relationships were healthier, I did have some that were emotionally abusive in that they were characterized by frequent put-downs, derogatory comments, and/or sexual coercion. Because I hadn't healed yet or become aware of the warning signs, I didn't recognize the signs of abuse and stop the cycle of unhealthy relationships. Thankfully, I never again got involved in a relationship involving physical abuse.

- In addition to learning what elements make a relationship healthy, it's equally important for survivors to learn how to identify the warning signs of unhealthy relationships so they can avoid them in the future. (I'll cover these in detail in part two of this book.)

2. **Help them assess what is important to them, the type of person they want to be, and the kinds of friends they want to have.**

- I missed out on many activities while dating Brock because of his "rules" and jealousy. So, after the breakup, I jumped into making up for lost time. I really didn't stop to consider what my values were, what I wanted for my life, which activities might be important to me, or what I wanted to be (or not be) involved in. So, for example, within a few weeks, I had a new boyfriend. This is a common pattern among survivors, with many quickly jumping into new relationships, and unfortunately often repeating the cycle of dating abusive partners. Thankfully, my first boyfriend after Brock wasn't abusive, but he did pressure me for sex. When I wouldn't give in, he returned to his former girlfriend, who would have sex with him.

· I also leapt into all kinds of social situations in order to engage in what I perceived to be "normal" teen and college activities that I thought I had missed out on in high school and my freshman year of college. I didn't drink alcohol while dating Brock, and despite seeing him at his worst when he was drunk, I began to experiment with alcohol. Although I went to my classes, I didn't end up studying as well as I should have. Instead, my priority was to never turn down an opportunity to do something outside of class, like hang out with new friends, go for a joy ride, or go to a party. This resulted in my grades suffering to the point that I was almost kicked out of college.

3. **Teach them that part of healing is learning what it means to be a survivor and potentially changing unhealthy mindsets.** Victims and survivors of abuse become accustomed to unhealthy mindsets, such as victim mentality or learned helplessness.

    Victim mentality is the outlook of a person who has been hurt and believes that others or current circumstances are the cause of the pain or discomfort they're feeling. When difficult situations occur, a person with a victim mentality sees the world as "unfair" and doesn't recognize that challenging, even painful, circumstances can sometimes be avoided. Thus, they fail to develop healthy coping skills and instead view themselves as unable to escape or avoid hardships.

    Henrik Edberg, a journalist who focuses on personal development, describes the mindset this way: "One big problem a lot of people have is that they slip into thinking of themselves as victims that have little or no control over their lives. In this headspace, you feel sorry for yourself, the world seems to be against you, and you get stuck. Little to no action is taken, and you get lost in a funk of sadness and self-pity."[2]

If the "victim" doesn't heal from this mindset, they don't realize they have the ability to influence or change a situation's outcome.

Similarly, learned helplessness occurs when a person feels helpless when it comes to avoiding negative situations. This is because previous experience has shown them that they do not have control.[3] They don't realize there are coping skills they can learn and ways to get beyond negative situations.

In my own experience, I didn't recognize and start to change my victim mentality until several years after dating Brock, when I found myself unhappy in an emotionally abusive relationship. I was feeling sorry for myself, and I kept wondering, *Why does he treat me this way?* One day I went for a walk to think things through. At first, I kept wishing someone in our lives—one of his parents, a friend, *anyone*—would recognize that his actions toward me were hurtful and would try to make him stop. But while praying to God and asking Him why my boyfriend treated me this way, I recognized for the first time that I was acting like a victim, and I didn't like it. I didn't want to be a victim.

That was a turning point! I suddenly realized I could make decisions to improve my situation; I didn't have to sit back, accept hurtful actions, and continue to be a victim. Instead of wishing *he* would change, *I* could change.

Chapter 12
"When did you forgive?"
Letting Go

Once I started talking openly about my high school relationship, someone asked me how long it took me to forgive Brock. Well, I had to stop and think.

Although Brock had hurt me on so many levels and in so many ways, I believed that his lies and his actions were *reactions* to things *I* had done wrong. While we were dating, I never thought what he did was his fault. I believed Brock had learned from his dad's behavior toward his mom and had even received similar treatment himself. Honestly, as each incident occurred, I was so relieved when the eruption ended with his explanation and apology, I think I genuinely forgave him each time.

The night I broke up with Brock, I was bold and desired justice. When he didn't strike me that night and the relationship was over, I didn't think about forgiveness; I just wanted him out of my life and needed to move forward.

It wasn't until someone asked me about forgiving him that I even thought about it. By this time, I had learned that

Brock could have chosen to treat me differently. But it was so many years later that the realization that he'd had a choice was more of a simple fact than something that made me angry. I realized I hadn't ever been angry with Brock or held him accountable in a way that required my forgiving him. I had let go of any resentment and was focused on healing.

Surprisingly, though, years after the breakup I did become angry with others in my life, and I had to work on understanding and forgiving them. I guess I wanted to blame someone else for what had happened to me, and so, briefly I was upset with my parents for not helping me get out of the relationship back when I was in high school.

But as much as I wished they'd been able to help me, I also recognized that I had pushed them away. While with Brock, I became increasingly ashamed that I was in an abusive relationship. So, when my parents did try to approach me about it, I pushed them away and ran straight into Brock's waiting arms.

As my parents grew increasingly concerned about what was going on, they tried to limit my time with him. I recall them encouraging me to spend more time with my friends, and later they began saying no to some of my plans with Brock. But whenever that happened, I rebelled against my parents' discipline and concern. I began to lie, telling them I was with friends but really spending the time with Brock. Each time my parents tried to intercede, I pushed them away, became defensive about the relationship, and drew closer to Brock.

My parents' inability to help get me away from Brock didn't stem from a lack of desire on their part to help me. It stemmed from my lack of willingness to be helped. Back in the 1980s, there wasn't much information or resources readily available about abusive relationships. My parents wanted to help but often didn't know how. They were also in a lonely, scary, uninformed place during my relationship with Brock; the resources and organizations that could assist teenage abuse victims and their families were hard to find and access. While violence in dating relationships is still barely talked about today, now there are organizations that exist for the sole purpose of bringing about change, and the knowledge and information readily available on the internet has made it easier to discover resources and guidance. Once I recognized the obstacles my parents experienced in their efforts to help me, I let go of the anger.

As I looked back on the relationship, trying to find junctures when someone could have helped me, I recognized no one truly could have done so because I was too ashamed to accept help. I also realized that the only reason I was able to break up with Brock and *stay away* from him was that I was the one who decided to leave.

As I reflected and processed, I became quite disappointed with myself over the poor decisions I'd made while in that relationship. My parents had taught me the difference between right and wrong. They had taught me to have integrity, and to have good values like honesty, kindness, and helping others. Yet I had allowed negative messages to influence me rather than standing up to those messages and going with what I knew to be right.

For example, I had bowed to peer pressure because I wanted to fit in and be like everybody else. When I overheard conversations in school that reinforced the message "Everyone else is doing it" (such as having a boyfriend and/or having sex), it influenced me. Instead, I should have taken time to think about my choices and actions. I should have chosen what was right for me and risked suffering what I perceived to be negative consequences, such as saying no to premarital sex and risking my boyfriend dumping me.

Would you believe that when I first spoke to a group of other adults almost twenty-five years after high school, I still carried shame from that decision? It was so very difficult to look in my audience's eyes while admitting I'd had premarital sex. Clearly, that choice was not one I should have made.

I was also ashamed of how I treated and pulled away from my family and friends. I'm so grateful for my high school friends who forgave me and accepted me with open arms, and for my family for being so understanding. As I continued to learn, grow, heal, and reflect, I discovered I needed to forgive myself for not making better choices and for straying from God's path for my life.

Managing Thoughts and Actions

I also needed to grow emotionally. Without realizing it, believing my situation resulted from someone else's actions or lack of actions was a filter I applied to my life for decades. Steeped in that victim mentality, I felt that things were done *to* me. It took me twenty years to understand that I have a choice in relationships. At last I learned the difference between external and internal management.

External management comes into play when we feel impacted by people or situations around us (such as, "I'm grumpy because she was rude to me"). Internal management occurs when we understand that others can't *make* us feel a certain way, and we realize the actions we take can affect the outcome in most situations. In other words, when we operate by internal management, we are taking ownership of our thoughts and actions.

I had developed an external habit of blaming others while overlooking my own skewed thoughts and perceptions. I grew to understand that, by assessing the situation and determining what actions I can take, I can influence the outcome. Thus, over time I started to realize my life experiences were not solely the result of someone else's decisions or actions.

If We Hold On to Anger

I once heard someone say, "Anger is like a poison you want to give someone else, but you swallow yourself." Anger keeps us in a negative place. In the past, when someone hurt me, it was easy to hold on to angry and resentful feelings. The hurt stayed with me, and I rolled it over in my mind, replaying the hurtful action or words and thereby allowing that pain to grow.

But holding on to anger hurts us and those around us more than the original real or perceived injustice. Let me explain.

If a friend hurts me, holding on to my anger distances me from them, making it harder to talk to them kindly the next time I see them. Holding on to my anger also affects those around me, because as I stew over the problem, I'm often irritable or low on patience with others. I'm distracted too by the unhealthy thoughts in my mind, and I can miss the joy right in front of me! I don't notice and appreciate the beauty of that flower, or the sparkling hues of the sunlight on water. Plus, if I choose to share my hurt and anger with someone else, I often cast the "offender" in a negative light, and my lamenting and complaining negatively impacts the person listening to me as well.

Anger hurts all of us. Realizing I'd developed the habit of external management helped me begin to shift to internal control. I started pausing to consider my thoughts and actions rather than just reacting.

Treating Others Right

As I've had these "aha!" moments, I've often wondered what type of person I would be if I were diagnosed with cancer. I know the old me would wallow in self-pity and lash out at those I care about because of the pain or fear over my diagnosis. I would justify my actions with thoughts like, *I have cancer; can't they see I'm in pain or suffering?* or *Why are they bothering me over this or that?*

This isn't how I want to treat those around me today. As a parent, it would kill me to instill a sense of sadness in my children because I couldn't control my anger and took it out on them. I feel the same about friends and family members; I have no desire to make the others around me miserable or hurt.

I'm thankful that I'm growing into a different person and hopefully treating others with kindness regardless of my circumstances.

All these thoughts led me to discover not only that I needed to let go of blaming societal influences for my decision to date and have sex with Brock, but also that I had to forgive myself for not making better choices and for straying from God's path for my life.

PART TWO

BECOMING AWARE OF AND PROTECTING OUR KIDS FROM NEGATIVE INFLUENCES

Chapter 13
Warning Signs of Unhealthy Relationships

Any relationship can range from healthy to abusive. By being aware of the characteristics of a dating relationship, we can determine whether signs indicate that the relationship is predominantly healthy, unhealthy, or abusive.

In healthy relationships, the partners will most often have feelings of happiness and contentment. The couple is comfortable with one another and secure in the relationship. Even a healthy relationship can have unhealthy components at times (such as when a disagreement escalates and one or both partners begin using hurtful words). But unhealthy components shouldn't arise often.

The relationship can be unhealthy when there are more unhealthy than healthy characteristics. Some relationships can be unhealthy without being or becoming abusive. For instance, one or both partners may be experiencing tension, feel they are being disrespected, or not feel comfortable being themselves.

Abusive relationships occur when one person uses unhealthy or increasingly excessive, negative behaviors to manipulate and exert control over the other person. These relationships often make one person feel insecure, stressed, cautious, and/or sad.

It's important for parents and other responsible and caring adults to recognize the signs of an unhealthy relationship so they can help today's youth avoid or end an abusive relationship.

Below, and on the following pages, are some of the warning signs that both you and your adolescents need to know and discuss.[1]

Is Someone I Know in a Relationship That Is Unhealthy or Abusive?

Characteristics of an unhealthy relationship include when someone in the relationship

- ignores or doesn't care about the other person's feelings;
- does not respect their partner's feelings, ideas, beliefs, or values;
- isn't comfortable sharing their feelings;
- avoids discussing issues in the relationship;

- is not willing to compromise;
- is suspicious or jealous;
- lies to the other person;
- spends most of their time with the other and has no outside interests or friends;
- gets upset easily;
- escalates disagreements into fights; and/or
- uses a loud voice, as well as harsh words or insults, in order to hurt the other person.

Below are some of the most common signs a partner may display in an abusive relationship:

- Gets angry when one person doesn't "drop everything" for the other person
- Criticizes the way the other person dresses
- Tells the other person they'll never find anyone else who wants to date them
- Keeps the other person from seeing friends or talking to other people—guys or girls
- Wants the other to quit a healthy activity they enjoy
- Tries to force the other person to go further sexually than they want to
- Checks the other person's cell phone or email without their permission
- Calls the other person demeaning names and puts them down (e.g., "You're stupid," "You can't do

anything right," "You're such a baby," "You're a slob," etc.), then laughs and says they were "only kidding" or that the other person is "too sensitive"
- Displays extreme jealousy, possessiveness, or insecurity
- Has an explosive temper (sudden, volatile outbursts and/or screaming at the other person)
- Isolates the other person from their family and/or friends
- Makes false accusations
- Has mood swings (their emotions change quickly, such as from happy to angry, laid back to irritable, or romantic to distant and cold)
- Tells the other person what to do rather than allowing them to make their own decisions and choices
- Raises a hand to the other person when angry, as if they're about to hit them
- Physically hurts the other person in any way

These aren't the only signs that can characterize an abusive relationship. Following are some signs that researchers have found could indicate an abusive relationship, although not always. It's important to realize that normally these signs are ones that the other person in the relationship may recognize. *Those who are outside the relationship may not be knowledgeable about the existence of these signs.*

The potential abuser

- wants to get serious in the relationship quickly;
- won't take *no* for an answer;
- is extremely critical of their partner, but can also extend that criticism to anyone in their own or their partner's life (peers, friends, family, teachers, etc.);
- wants to make all the decisions in the relationship;
- dismisses other people's opinions and feelings;
- puts constant pressure on the other person;
- demands to know where the other person is all the time;
- uses guilt trips ("If you really loved me, you would . . .");
- feels they deserve unconditional love and support;
- has a history of bad relationships;
- blames the other person for their feelings and actions ("You asked for it" or "You made me mad!"); and/or
- apologizes for their violent behavior and promises not to do it again—but the promise is temporary, and the behavior will be repeated in the future, often many times.

How Someone in an Abusive Relationship May Change Over Time

For parents, teachers, neighbors, and friends, here are some additional signs that you, as a person outside the relationship, may observe in the person being abused, or in the abuser. Once the teenager enters the relationship and starts being abused, they

- are no longer as outgoing and instead have become withdrawn, depressed, and/or anxious; they also may frequently cry;
- are less likely to be as involved as they were in school activities or places of worship;
- stop spending time with other friends and family;
- become critical of their own appearance, talents, or abilities;
- change the way they use technology; maybe they're not on social media anymore, or they get upset if they're asked to turn off their phone;
- become secretive; for example, they may provide only vague details about their plans, or stop talking about their partner with family and friends;
- stop getting "good grades," or allow their grades to decline from where they used to be;
- change the way they dress; also, they may wear clothing that doesn't match the season (e.g., they used to dress trendy and now dress much more

conservatively, or they wear long sleeves in the summertime);

- have unexplained bruises or injuries, or if they do offer an explanation for an injury, their explanation doesn't make sense (e.g., ran into a door, tripped on a curb, etc.);
- become protective of their phone or computer;
- apologize and/or make excuses for their partner's behavior; for example, if their partner is sullen, rude, cold, or abrasive, the victim in the relationship may say the abuser is just "having a bad day";
- frequently have to explain why they did what they did to their partner or often say they're "sorry" to their partner;
- are jumpy at the sound of a loud or sudden noise, or instinctively shrink away when another person is loud or unexpectedly moves close to them; and/or
- mention their partner's violent behavior but then laugh it off as if it's a joke.

Signs to Help You Identify Someone Who's an Abuser

As for the signs of an abuser that parents, teachers, youth directors, and peers can learn to recognize, they can include the following. An abuser

- roughhouses or play-wrestles with their partner;
- may come from a tragic home life in which they are verbally demeaned and/or physically abused, and in which one or both of their parents are alcoholics or use drugs;
- is likely to be aggressive in other areas of their life: they may put their fist through walls or closets when enraged, bang their fists to make a point, or throw things when angry;
- frequently gives unsolicited or critical "advice" about their partner's choice of friends, hairstyle, clothes, or makeup;
- emails or texts their dating partner excessively, sometimes at all times of the day or night;
- tells their partner "I love you" early in the relationship;
- becomes jealous if their partner merely looks at or speaks casually with someone of the opposite sex;
- drinks or uses drugs; and/or
- abuses other people or animals.

It's important that we take the time to not just read these lists but retain them so we will be able to recognize any of these signs if they occur in the life of a teen we know. As we've learned, abuse happens to an alarming number of our youth, and most often the abuse is hidden and undisclosed by those involved.

Of course, it is the most helpful to begin talking about these warning signs with our children or other youth in our lives *before* they begin dating. But even if they've already started dating, reviewing these lists with them at any time is still beneficial. Remaining vigilant in reviewing these lists and discussing them with others can help save a teen!

Chapter 14

What to Say, What to Do:
Helping a Teen If You Suspect Abuse

It doesn't matter whether someone is being subjected to verbal, emotional, physical, or sexual abuse, no one deserves to be mistreated in this way, and **no one should harm a partner this way**. Everyone deserves healthy, respectful relationships.

If you suspect that someone you know may be in an abusive relationship, talk to them in the following manner:

1. **When you approach the person, be gentle, supportive, and understanding as you bring up this delicate and unsettling topic.** Remember, discussing the possibility that they are a victim of abuse and that their relationship is abusive is probably going to be hard on the young person you're trying to help. Most likely, they will be feeling scared, embarrassed, ashamed, and/or defensive. So, remind them you care about them and want to help.

And reassure them that *you don't think this is their fault.*[1] Some examples of how you might start a sensitive conversation on this topic:

- **If you haven't already discussed the warning signs with them,** start the conversation neutrally with something like, "A friend recently gave me a list of warning signs of an abusive relationship, and I wanted to share it with you in case it can help anyone you know. It seems that unhealthy traits are revealed slowly and subtly. It's possible for someone to find themselves in an unhealthy or abusive relationship without recognizing the warning signs. If you ever find yourself in a relationship like this, please know I care about you and am here to help. If it turns out you're concerned about the way your relationship is going, I hope you'll talk with me about it."

- **If you've observed warning signs, you could say,** "I care about you and have noticed a difference in your relationship with X. Are they treating you respectfully (kindly, etc.)?"

- **If you've witnessed an unhealthy interaction or bruises, you might begin with,** "I'm concerned and want what's best for you. Sometimes people can be going through a difficult time and take it out on us. While it's okay to talk their frustration through, it's not okay to take it out on us. Have X's behaviors or actions changed in a way that hurts you?"

It's also important to remember that the abuser has regularly acted superior and talked down to the other person. Be careful not to come across as more intelligent or wise than the youth and avoid statements that could convey you believe that this never would have happened to you. Doing so could inadvertently confirm exactly what their abuser has been telling them.[2]

2. **Listen more than talk once you've broached the topic and the victim or survivor starts acknowledging the existence of abuse.** Assess their comfort level, and if you think they feel comfortable with your doing so, ask some gentle questions. In preparation for the conversation, you may want to obtain a handout that lists the warning signs of abuse. If you think the person might be receptive, hand the material to them. Even if they aren't saying much during the initial conversation with you, *reading over the warning signs may help them realize they're being abused and don't deserve to be treated this way.*

Know too that it might be easier for them to talk to a stranger, so make sure the resource you provide includes a phone number and other resources for help. It's especially important to ensure that the material includes safety information, such as how to call the resource from someone else's phone.

3. **Believe the victim and show that you take seriously whatever they share with you.** They may be reluctant to reveal their experiences for fear that no one will believe what they say. So, validate their feelings and show your support. With time they may become comfortable sharing even more information.

    Be careful not to underestimate the intensity of their situation due to age, dating inexperience, or the length of the relationship.

4. **Be patient.** It may take them some time to be ready to leave the relationship.

    As much as they probably want the abuse to end, they also have strong feelings for the other person, and any breakup is difficult. It may also take time for them to trust others. Since control is a component of dating violence, the abuser has most likely instilled in them a distrust of others, even of their parents, family, or friends. They probably feel very isolated.

5. **Develop a safety plan.** Whether the victim is ready to leave the relationship or not, help them develop a plan for staying safe, such as avoiding the kitchen (which has knives), avoiding being alone with the abusive person, and knowing how to reach help if needed.[3] Brainstorming can help them think through potential scenarios and come up with strategies to sidestep or escape potentially dangerous situations. When the victim is ready to leave the relationship, it will be even more critical to have thought through a safety plan. One of the most dangerous times in an abusive relationship is when the victim decides to leave (see chapter 10). **Violent behavior often escalates during a breakup or in the weeks and months immediately afterward.**

6. **After checking whether the victim is comfortable with your doing so, consider contacting their school and asking about its policy regarding dating violence.** The school may have provisions in place that could confidentially help the victim. Let the victim know that, before providing the school officials with any names, you will ask questions about the school's privacy policy and about how many and which staff would be notified. When asking the victim for their approval to contact the school, also check if there's any additional information the victim would like to know from the school when you contact them.

Ultimately, the person being abused must be the one who decides to leave the relationship. There are many complex reasons victims stay in unhealthy relationships, but extending your support can make a critical difference in helping the victim decide to end the harmful bond.[4] I wholeheartedly encourage you to carefully, gently, and thoughtfully take this step. It can prevent intense despair, fear, or isolation in the life—and quite possibly save the life—of someone you care about.

Does Intervention Work?

It may not be easy to convince the victim or the abuser to receive the help they need. Studies have shown that once the abuse has started, intervention is often minimally effective. Why is this?

- **For perpetrators of dating violence:** Most believe they're not doing anything wrong and that what has happened to their victim is not their fault. They prefer a controlling and manipulative relationship, even finding it beneficial, and are resistant to changing their behavior.
- **For victims of abuse:** Once abuse has started, the victim is so enmeshed in the cycle of control they

feel guilty for leaving their partner—or believe this is what love is—and so are not ready to leave the relationship.

So, what works best? According to a study by Carlos Cuevas, a professor of criminology and criminal justice who codirects the Violence and Justice Research Lab at Northeastern University, **engaging parents to help with prevention is very beneficial for decreasing dating violence**. Cuevas concluded, "We think family education is one of the real gateways for intervention and prevention. If you are able to educate families and parents around these issues, it provides *the first line of defense for helping kids avoid getting into these kinds of behaviors*".[5]

Educating ourselves and our community is one of the most effective ways to change the cycle of abuse. **For both the victim and the abuser, awareness and prevention have the best results in decreasing violence in teen dating relationships.**

The following chapters will cover the elements of our society that can negatively influence our children to choose risky behaviors, as well as what we can do to help prevent them from getting involved in these behaviors.

Chapter 15
Too Much Too Soon:
Media Influence

I grew up in Texas, and most summers my family was fortunate to be invited to our neighbors' beach house for a few weeks. The five-hour drive stretched through a desolate section of south Texas with only a few occasional gas stations along the way. Once we entered the final hour of the drive, we had to turn onto a road with an excruciating speed limit of only thirty miles per hour. Eventually, though, the scenery changed as palm trees started to line the roads, and we began to see glimpses of the bay before crossing the bridge to the beach.

My excitement and anticipation of the beach vacation increased significantly as the first few palm trees came into sight. Today, even when driving to the beach as an adult, I continue to get excited and anticipate the beach as soon as I begin to see palm trees.

Fast-forward to the time my sister accepted a job in Miami. During a trip to visit her, I took all four of our kids to the beach for an afternoon. When we arrived there for the first time, I thought it was a bit odd to see palm trees growing sporadically here and there in the parking lot and then on the beach. While I'd seen plenty of palm trees when I was growing up, I'd never seen one actually on the beach. I enjoyed seeing them so close and didn't pause to think about why these trees were placed in random spots, so different from the growing pattern of those I'd seen when I was young.

A few months after my visit to Miami, I had to travel to the towns near the beach in south Texas. As I got close and saw the neat rows of palm trees lining the highway shoulder, it suddenly dawned on me that these trees were transplanted!

While palm trees may grow naturally in some tropical locations, like Miami, I had grown up accepting the false perception that palm trees grow organically, in neat little rows, as I'd seen them in south Texas.

> It can be hard to discern the truth when the clues aren't obvious, or when we don't have the wisdom to see through an illusion or deception.

Only when I began researching the information for the next few chapters of this book and reflected on the decisions of my youth and potential influences did I come to see how easily I'd accepted the unhealthy behaviors and relationships that surrounded me as a child. They were all around me, so they felt "normal." I started to see things differently only when I applied the "palm tree concept" to the TV shows, song lyrics, video games, and magazine covers that had long been part of my environment.

As I thought hard about the messages I received as a youth and learned how those messages could influence me, I became angry at a world that allowed TV and music to contain messages that aren't appropriate for teenage ears and eyes.

Through media sources, teens are exposed to messages about sex, drinking, drugs, and violence. But can these messages really influence our kids' behavior? Many studies present results that say yes.

Before we dive into exactly what those studies have revealed, let's consider what the advertisers are trying to teach us through the lens of commercials.

One morning I was watching a commercial that showed a man driving a car. As he drives, he pushes the Bluetooth button and tells the car, "Play 'Can't Touch This.'" Instantly, M. C. Hammer's song "Can't Touch This" begins playing in the car. Before the song ends, the man says, "Play 'I've Got Eyes Everywhere,'" and we hear the car switch to the soundtrack by T-Booth and the Sensations. Next, he instructs Bluetooth, "Play 'Keep Your Hands to Yourself,'" and the music immediately changes to the song by the Georgia Satellites. The car then comes to a stop, and you see the man turn toward the backseat. The viewer sees his daughter sitting in the backseat of the car with her date. Based on the clothes the teens are wearing and the music coming from the building they've pulled up in front of, it appears they're going to a school dance. As they begin to leave the car, the girl says to her father, "We get it, Dad." As a parent, I related and found much humor in the commercial.[1]

Several hours later, the commercial was still on my mind. It continued to bring a grin to my face as I thought about the message the dad had been sending his teen daughter and her date. As the commercial kept circling back in my head, I decided to find a link to a video of the commercial to post and share with my friends on Facebook.

Commercials make an impression on their viewers, and they frequently impact the choices we make, whether it's buying a new product or trying a new restaurant. In a poll from September 2013, 68 percent of the respondents indicated that they "always" or "sometimes" took action as a result of a TV ad.[2] Another survey found that TV ads were the most effective form of advertising to college students.[3]

Consider this: Most commercials are only fifteen to sixty seconds long, yet they have a substantial impact on us. So, what does that say about the influence of television shows and movie content? Television shows, not counting the commercials, tend to be an average of twenty to forty-three minutes long, and of course, movies are even longer. **If an ad on TV can impact our decision-making 68 percent of the time, consider how much more a television show or movie can influence our perceptions and decisions.**

James Steyer, the founder and CEO of Common Sense Media, has shared that

> children's screen time has wide-ranging impli-cations for their social and emotional development, how they form relationships, how they identify themselves, and how they are exposed to . . . hate speech.[4]

Add to this the fact that a 2021 survey by Common Sense Media found that in 2019, teens spent **almost 7.5 hours each day** watching TV, movies, and online videos, playing video games, and visiting social media sites. (In 2021, time spent on these media sources increased by over an hour per day.)[5]

Suffice it to say, our kids can easily be saturated with media messages. It's helpful if parents instill household rules about their kids' media use. Kids who adhere to such rules consume three hours less per day.[6] To help guide parents and other guardians on what type of rules might be set, the American Academy of Pediatrics has established guidelines for children, rules that can easily be used to guide tweens and teens as well. Here are some of the guidelines:[7]

- Turn off devices at least one hour before bed (the blue light emitted by mobile devices makes it harder to get to sleep).
- Create screen-free times and zones (such as no phones while eating or in the child's room during the night).
- View online videos, television shows, and movies with your kids. (This keeps the parent connected to what the child is interested in and opens the door to discussing the content with them.)

Another article, "The Influence of Media Violence on Youth," shared study findings showing that when parents speak against violence on TV "or restrict viewing of violent content, children place less importance on violent programs and have less aggressive attitudes."[8]

Media messages might not *make* us engage in risky behavior, but they can certainly *influence* our decisions. When we don't know how they can influence us and we don't take the time to stop to decide whether we want this influence in our lives or the lives of our children, we can easily be led astray.

In his book *Age of Opportunity*, Paul David Tripp shares a piece of advice he regularly gives his children, "There's a war out there . . . Be careful, be aware of the battle. Don't forget there is a scheming enemy out there who is out to deceive, divide, and destroy."[9] He doesn't mean an actual war, like we hear about on the news or learn about in history class in school. He means **the war for our souls**.

To prepare for the fight, we need to arm ourselves with knowledge and truth. So, over the next few chapters, we'll explore

- the sources of the messages that surround our kids,
- how these messages can potentially impact them,
- how to guide and protect them so they avoid making risky choices, and
- ideas to teach them to make healthy choices and use media in positive ways.

Chapter 16

Television and the Movies:
What They're Showing Our Kids

As a toddler, I remember weaving between my parents' legs when my dad arrived home from work and greeted my mom with a kiss. As I grew older, I watched them hold hands, help each other around the house, and go on dates. By observing my parents' relationship and those of my friends' parents, I was learning about romantic relationships. But unfortunately, as I grew up, I learned more about dating and relationships from TV shows, movies, and song lyrics.

The Love Boat debuted on TV when I was eight, and soon it was making a big impression on my young mind. As a new *Love Boat* episode began each week, strangers boarded the cruise ship, and by the end of the hour, a new romance had blossomed and the lovestruck couple departed the ship arm in arm. As I watched the show week after week, I began to dream of a romantic relationship like the ones that happened so easily on TV.

More than thirty years later, I look back at this memory and wonder, *Really? Did I really start dreaming about dating and love at the age of eight?* The adult side of me says an eight-year-old is too young to know what love is and too young to want romantic love. But looking back, I recall how sincere my feelings were at the time.

As I continued to spend many hours each week during my childhood watching TV, numerous shows helped mold my thoughts and desire for a romantic relationship. I remember watching *Gilligan's Island,* and while I was intrigued with life on the island and the creative plots the castaways came up with in their attempts to be rescued, I also tried to understand the difference between the sultry Ginger character and what seemed to be the less-desirable-to-men character of good girl Mary Ann.

The men on the show simply fell over themselves to help Ginger! Over the course of the show, there was some romantic interest in Mary Ann, but most of the time she didn't have quite the same effect on the men. I really liked Mary Ann; she was sweet and down to earth. I wondered what was wrong with a girl like Mary Ann (and potentially me). Although I didn't understand sex yet, it was easy to see and perceive the physical appeal Ginger had to men and observe what Mary Ann seemed to be lacking in that area.

Happy Days was another show that taught me about dating relationships. Over the years I watched the character of Richie develop from an awkward teen trying to be cool around girls to a young man falling in love with Mary Beth and "finding his thrill on Blueberry Hill." But Henry Winkler's character of Fonzie was the ultimate relationship teacher. He was a mystery—aloof and independent while also being a good friend. He was the cool guy, and girls flocked to him. All he had to do was snap his fingers (literally!) and a girl (or two) would be on his arm. I never stopped to wonder why a girl would jump for someone who snapped his fingers to get her attention, or why she would want to be with him for a week, a day, or even just a night before he moved on to the next girl. The "cool" factor made him desirable. Rather than grasping that being with Fonzie wouldn't make for a good relationship, I wanted to grow up and look like one of the girls on his arm.

Three's Company pitted the average Janet against the dim-witted but beautiful and sexy Chrissy. While the show included themes about friendship, what stood out to me was Janet's experiences, or lack of dating experiences, against Chrissy's ability to attract men and always have a date. It was perplexing. Although I didn't want to be ditzy and taken advantage of like Chrissy always was, I also didn't want to be ignored by guys like Janet was.

I didn't realize it at the time, but in addition to forming thoughts about dating relationships, I was also forming opinions of myself and how I wanted to appear based on what the media presented. I learned about how to act and not act, how to dress and what not to wear, and what was desirable and what wasn't from guys' point of view. I was learning about sex appeal too—a message that became abundantly clear in the movie *Grease*.

I loved the movie *Grease* and wanted to be Sandy. I think every girl did at some point—she was beautiful, sweet, and in love with handsome Danny. I was also about eight years old when *Grease* debuted in movie theaters, and while I didn't understand everything portrayed in the movie the first time I saw it, I did comprehend that as a "good girl," Sandy wasn't enough for Danny. In fact, the "good" characters weren't respected by their peers, were the brunt of many jokes, and were easily dismissed by others. I was learning from *Grease* that it wasn't acceptable to be "good."

Fast-forward thirty years to when my daughter was about eight years old. *Grease* aired on TV, and I was excited to share a fun movie with her. As we watched it together, she loved the singing and dancing! But seeing the movie through a mother's eyes for the first time, I was dismayed by the messages I was putting in front of my daughter. As the years went by, I was increasingly uncomfortable when we came across the movie on TV, and I found myself steering her away from it. As an adult, the messages it conveyed about dating relationships really concerned me.

In the movie, although Sandy and Danny enjoyed time together over the summer, once they are back at school, he doesn't treat her very well because he feels it's more important to maintain his image as a "cool guy" in front of his friends. Eventually, he does ask her out and takes her on a date, only to try to hide it from his friends because she's sweet and intelligent, not sexy and putting out. Despite this treatment, Sandy continues to place herself near Danny, hoping to capture his attention. As a young girl watching the dilemmas unfold while still remembering the happy relationship they had at the beginning of the movie, I always hoped they'd get back together. But I never stopped to consider why Sandy liked Danny and continued to give him chances throughout the year. I never wondered, *At what point does she decide he doesn't treat her right and isn't the guy for her?* Instead, I learned that the "good girl" loses the guy every time.

This message is emphasized in the second-to-last scene when Sandy's friend asks her, "Sandy, are you happy?" and Sandy responds, "No, but I know how to be." In the next scene we see Sandy wearing tight clothes, high heels, and red lipstick—and she's smoking too! When Danny sees her, not only does she immediately win his attention, but he also now falls all over himself to be with her. It's suddenly "cool" to follow this girl, because she's "hot." So, what did I learn? That the good girl has to change and must look and act sexy if she wants to get the guy. As an adult I recognized this is unhealthy, but as a child and teen, I grasped the message that I had to be sexy in order to be accepted.

A few years later, when my daughter was thirteen, I took her and a friend to see the movie *The Fault in Our Stars*. This is a wonderful story that not only gives the viewer a glimpse into living with cancer and teaches them about compassion, but also shows a mutually respectful, caring, and thoughtful teen dating relationship.

But . . . both the book and the movie have one small section in which the dating teens head back to one of their hotel rooms and have sex while visiting Amsterdam. While it's a brief part of the storyline and doesn't go into much detail, it's still more than a thirteen-year-old should be exposed to—not because I'm naïve or want my daughter to be sheltered, but because at age thirteen, she doesn't need that visualization!

As we watched the PG-13 movie, I cringed as my daughter witnessed what should only be shared intimately between two people in marriage. Now she had a permanent stamp in her mind of what sex looks like and could replay it in her mind if she chose to.

I also ached for the teen actors. For their roles in the movie, they had to portray an intimate situation that should be private, exposing themselves publicly to entertain the viewer.

While talking with my daughter and her friend afterward, I felt like a prude as I said I didn't think that scene was necessary, and I thought the filmmakers took it "too far." Sadly, by today's standards, I am a prude—and that's my point.

We've Lowered the Bar

While there have been many television shows and movies that offer wonderful examples of family life and values, there are just as many, if not more, that have encouraged us to lower our values over the years, making things that were once unacceptable become acceptable.

> Moving from unacceptable to acceptable can be good when learning how to be resilient, correcting racial prejudices, or making other positive changes. But when it teaches us to accept premarital sex, violence, drinking, or other risky behaviors, we need to question what we and our kids are learning and whether we should be watching.

A 2005 study by the Kaiser Family Foundation (KFF) looked at programming across ten channels (ABC, CBS, NBC, Fox, PBS, Lifetime, TNT, USA, HBO, and one station that is an affiliate of the WB) from 4:00 a.m. to 9:00 p.m. EST.[1] It covered all genres, except daily newscasts, sports events, and children's shows. The study found a significant prevalence of sexual messages and content in American television:

- "Among the top twenty most watched shows by teens, 70% include some kind of sexual content, and nearly half (45%) include sexual behavior" (from passionate kissing to implied or depicted sexual activity). (The study didn't mention the names of the shows.)
- The top teen shows had **6.7 sex-related scenes per hour**.
- Seventy-seven percent of prime-time shows contained sexual content (talking about sex, and sexual behaviors).
- Ninety-two percent of movies had sexual content.

The KFF report went on to state that television contributes to a teen's sexual knowledge, beliefs, expectations, attitudes, and even behaviors. Specifically:

- "Nearly 75% of teens aged 15–17 indicated sex on TV influences the sexual behavior of kids their age."
- "12- to 17-year-olds that are heavy viewers of sexual content are *twice* as likely to initiate sexual intercourse over the next year as those that saw the least amount."
- "Exposure to *talking about sex on TV* was associated with the *same risks as exposure* to sexual behavior depictions."

In 2010 the Candie's Foundation partnered with *Seventeen* magazine to survey girls ages fourteen to eighteen to learn how these teens think the media influences teenage sex. Among the results:[2]

- Nearly half (48 percent) of teens surveyed obtained their information on sex from TV shows.
- More than half (55 percent) agreed that TV shows and movies encourage teenagers to have sex.

It's also concerning that while sexual content is prevalent in media, the storylines rarely mention the emotions, risks, or consequences (pregnancy, depression, STDs) that can arise from sexual activity and that can negatively impact a teen. It's also uncommon for the shows to mention how to stay safe while sexually active (i.e., by using a condom).[3]

Dr. Todd Huffman, a pediatrician, shares:

The sexual content in much of the media today's teens attend to is frequent, glamorized, and consequence free. "Everyone does it" on television and in the movies, or so it seems, yet the need for birth control, the risks of pregnancy or sexually transmitted infections, and the need for responsibility are rarely discussed.[4]

Remarkably, studies have found that *teens who watch shows with a storyline about safer sex or the consequences of sexual activity are less likely to engage in sexual activity.* However, KFF found that only 11 percent of shows portray this type of storyline; and while sexual content has increased over the years, *instances of the message about safe sex have remained low.*[5]

In summary, many studies and reports show a con= tinued prevalence of sexual content in movies and television (and it continues to increase over time) and that these themes influence our children's decisions about sexual activity.

Don't Dismiss Too Easily

While parents, educators, and others are aware that some middle and junior high school students across the United States have become sexually active, we often casually dismiss their choices as "Kids will be kids" or "They're curious."

I'd like us all to stop and ask ourselves, "What is causing children to become sexually active at earlier and earlier ages?" Is it *really* that they're curious or looking to engage in adventure or risks, or is it because of the increasingly graphic sexual content the media is putting in front of them at increasingly young ages?

Violence and the Media

In addition to sexual content, TV and movies often contain numerous depictions of violence, which also negatively influence our society.

When an extreme case of violence, such as a school shooting, occurs, news reports often include speculation about how violence in TV and movies may affect our children and teens. Doubters often dismiss the claims and speculation, proclaiming that what we see on TV can't actually influence us to be aggressive in real life. *But that's not the case.* Scientific studies have concluded that violence viewed on TV can influence our own everyday behavior and that of our youth.

Television began arriving in American homes in the 1940s, and by the 1950s Americans were expressing concern about the consequences violence in the media has on our children, youth, and communities.[6]

One small town in British Columbia provided a unique opportunity to study the effects television can have on a community.[7] This remote town (code-named Notel) did not have television access until 1973. Tannis MacBeth from the University of British Columbia had the foresight to study how exposure to television would affect this particular community.

The study looked at Notel and two other Canadian towns of similar size and demographics. The other two towns already had television in their communities. MacBeth measured several factors in children in all three communities before the introduction of television in Notel and then two years later.

The study concluded that watching television (even television with just one channel) was linked to the following results:[8]

- Verbal and physical aggression increased in all students.
    - It's especially interesting to note that aggression didn't just increase in the students who already displayed some aggression but also rose at the same rate in those who were not aggressive prior to watching television.
- Watching TV slowed down the learning process for reading. Children who took in more TV tended to fall behind in reading skills, while those who watched less tended to be stronger readers.
    - The disparity grew as the children got older. Those who didn't read well turned to TV more often, increasing the divide between them and children who read well.
- In adults, it took longer to solve problems, and they persevered less.
- Adults over the age of fifty-six were less likely to be engaged in community activities.

Thousands of studies were conducted over more than fifty years by reputable public health and medical organizations, including the Surgeon General's office and the National Institute of Mental Health. These studies all found that viewing violence in entertainment can increase aggressive attitudes and behaviors.

The American Academy of Pediatrics (AAP) report on media violence cited a study on TV violence in which researchers

> evaluated almost 10,000 hours of broadcast programming from 1995 through 1997 and revealed that 61% of the programming portrayed interpersonal violence, much of it in an entertaining or glamorized manner. The highest proportion of violence was found in children's shows. Of all animated feature films produced in the United States between 1937 and 1999, 100% portrayed violence, and the amount of violence with intent to injure has increased through the years.[9]

Furthermore, the *Children, Violence, and the Media* report noted that "by the age of 18 an American child will have seen 16,000 simulated murders and 200,000 acts of violence."[10]

At the Congressional Public Health Summit in 2000, six health organizations (the American Academy of Pediatrics, American Academy of Child and Adolescent Psychiatry, American Psychological Association, American Medical Association, American Academy of Family Physicians, and American Psychiatric Association) released a "Joint Statement on the Impact of Entertainment Violence on Children."[11] Below is an excerpt from the statement:[12]

> There are several measurable negative effects of children's exposure to violent entertainment. These effects take several forms:
>
> - Children who see a lot of violence are more likely to view violence as an effective way of settling conflicts. Children exposed to violence are more likely to assume that acts of violence are acceptable behavior.
> - Viewing violence can lead to emotional desensitization toward violence in real life. It can decrease the likelihood that one will take action on behalf of a victim when violence occurs.
> - Entertainment violence feeds a perception that the world is a violent and mean place. Viewing violence increases fear of becoming a victim of violence, with a resultant increase in self-protective behaviors and a mistrust of others.

  ° Viewing violence may lead to real-life violence. Children exposed to violent programming at a young age have a higher tendency for violent and aggressive behavior later in life than children who are not so exposed.

In short, TV violence impacts our children on many levels. While there are several factors that protect children and youth (such as connection to family and involvement in school, church, and/or the community), being exposed to violence in media can increase or lead to

- anger,
- desensitization to violence,
- fear of being harmed,
- depression,
- nightmares and trouble sleeping,
- aggressive thoughts,
- verbally and emotionally aggressive behavior, and/or
- thinking of violence as a means of solving problems.[13]

According to a 2003 report by the American Psychological Society, longitudinal studies have found that frequent exposure to violent media in childhood can lead to aggression later in life, including physical assaults and spousal abuse. The report summarized, "Research on violent television and films, video games, and music **reveals**

unequivocal evidence that media violence increases the likelihood of aggressive and violent behavior in both immediate and long-term contexts."[14]

As I read these research articles, I'm saddened that for decades the medical community has been studying and warning us of the negative impact that violent content in television, movies, and video games has on us, our children, and society; yet, instead of making changes for the better, violent content continues to increase, and many of us continue to watch it. But we can do better; we can turn away. Also, if ratings and profits shrink, that sends a message to the producers and all who benefit in the media industry, and hopefully, we can bring about positive change.

Changing It Up

When I was a child, I watched television shows like *Gunsmoke* and *Bonanza*. As a teenager, I remember enjoying the Freddy Krueger movies, starting with *A Nightmare on Elm Street*. As an adult, I've liked watching the stories unfold on *The Big Bang Theory*, *Two and a Half Men*, *Law & Order*, and *NCIS*. I've chosen to watch television shows with sexual and violent messages for as long as I can remember.

Then, soon after my first child was born, some friends and I watched a movie with a disturbing and violent storyline. The movie stayed with me for days and, for lack of a better word, made me feel yucky. As a new mom, I found I only wanted to think about positive things and started to pull away from violent shows.

So, I stopped following *Law & Order* but continued to watch others with slightly less disturbing storylines, like *NCIS* and *Blue Bloods*. I've also enjoyed shows like *Friends*, *Grey's Anatomy*, *Private Practice*, and *Desperate Housewives*—shows that, while fictional, still conveyed messages about lying, deceit, promiscuity, infidelity, drinking, and other negative behaviors.

I often recorded these shows and would catch up on them while I ran on the treadmill or after my kids had gone to bed. Occasionally my kids would come to ask me a question while I was on the treadmill, or other times they would have trouble sleeping and would come into my room while one of the shows was on. Sometimes an inappropriate scene would be playing at that exact moment, and my response was always panicked as I told them to close their eyes while I scrambled for the remote to pause the show. After my children returned to bed, I began to wonder what kind of example I was setting for my own children. Why was I watching shows with inappropriate content? Was being an adult enough of a justification for viewing these shows?

Then I heard a radio episode of *Focus on the Family*. In it, Paul and Virginia Friesen, parents to three daughters and founders of Home Improvement Ministries, said that when their children were small, they decided they would watch only shows they'd feel comfortable having their children see, even after their children had gone to bed. They made this decision so that, in case their children got up at night, they wouldn't feel like exciting things were going on after they'd gone to bed—things they might then look forward to being able to view when they got older![15]

The Friesens' beliefs opened my eyes. Not only were they setting a better example for their children, but they were also limiting negative media influences in their own lives. So, after hearing about this idea, I began to think more about making changes in my own life. I too wanted to stop watching shows with negative or unhealthy messages and set a better example for my kids.

But it was difficult at first! I felt connected to the shows and wanted to know what happened in the characters' lives the next week, and then the week after that. Nonetheless, I stopped recording shows like *Grey's Anatomy*, *Private Practice*, and *Desperate Housewives*, and within two weeks I found I didn't miss them the way I thought I would. But I still watched reruns of some other shows like *NCIS* on some weekends or *Blue Bloods* on Friday nights.

Then God nudged me to write this book. Like most busy adults with a job, kids to take care of, and a house to maintain, I was short on time. So, on the Saturdays my kids were with their dad, I started researching and writing my book in the mornings, then doing my chores in the afternoon before I'd "treat" myself to some TV—usually *NCIS* or *The Big Bang Theory*. I felt I deserved a break, and that watching a TV show would fulfill my need to relax. But I often spent more time watching TV than I'd meant to, and usually, I ended up neglecting other things that still needed to get done.

One Saturday afternoon when I grew tired and stopped writing, Jesus challenged me to deny myself and see what I could do with my time instead of watching TV. Guess what? I spent the next six hours getting two projects done!

Accomplishing those two projects that I always seemed to "never have enough time in the day to do" was a *huge* relief. It felt so good to have them done, and it also showed me I didn't need to spend my time watching TV. Not only did I not miss the shows, but I was more relaxed (often the drama-filled shows made me feel anxious), had positive thoughts filling my head (rather than negative messages from the shows), felt better because I didn't feel guilty about the time I had wasted in front of the TV, and had gotten a big project off my to-do list.

Occasionally I still watch some TV, but now instead of drama-filled shows, I turn to shows with a positive message. In case nothing I want to watch is on, I have DVDs of some of my favorites, including *Apollo 13*, *Greater*, *The Blind Side*, *Freedom Writers*, *Rudy*, *Gifted Hands*, *Hoosiers*, the *Love Comes Softly* series (to show my kids examples of healthy relationships), and boxed DVD sets of some of my kids' favorites, such as *Full House*.

Chapter 17

What Did That Song Just Say?
In a World of Unlimited Song Choice

In sixth grade, my friends and I loved the song "The Tide Is High" so much that we spent an entire afternoon writing down and memorizing all the lyrics—listening, rewinding, and listening again to make sure we had it right. (This was back when we had records and cassette players!)

The song is about a girl who wants to date a boy who, from the song lyrics, is apparently dating other girls. The girl singing the song declares she's going to hold on until she's his "number one," despite how the boy, presumably a dating partner, treats her. So, at the age of eleven, I was continuing to learn about romantic relationships, but the lyrics of this song were already teaching me that dating relationships aren't always healthy.

As I grew into a teen, I was trying to figure out who I was and how to act, and I also wanted to learn about relationships. I turned to songs to guide me. I related to the messages being sung and listened to them for advice. They taught me about love and longing, family relationships, and even rebellion in songs like "We're Not Gonna Take It," "Smokin' in the Boys Room," and "(You Gotta) Fight for Your Right (to Party)."

Some titles were enough on their own to convey a message to me, like "I Want to Know What Love Is," "Don't You Want Me?" "Addicted to Love," and "Keep On Loving You."

The lyrics in songs like "I Need You Tonight" and Madonna's "Like a Virgin" taught me more about love and sex. Then there were the more graphic songs like "You Shook Me All Night Long" and "Boom Boom Boom (Let's Go Back to My Room)." When sixteen-year-old singer Tiffany sang "I Think We're Alone Now," it was easy to relate that to my personal experiences and justify being alone with my high school boyfriend in his bedroom.

When I started high school, the majority of my class-mates shunned teen pregnancy. The few teens who attended school pregnant seemed to be outcasts. Then Madonna came out with "Papa Don't Preach," a song about "keeping my baby," and it made me stop and wonder: If Madonna was singing about it, was teen sex, even getting pregnant, as bad as all of us had originally perceived? Madonna not only addressed the issue head-on, bringing it out into the open, but she did so with rebellious pride.

Surround Sound

Almost as soon as our children are born, they're introduced to music. Parents and other caregivers may hum, play, or sing songs to them to convey feelings, express love, or help little ones fall asleep at night. As babies turn into toddlers, adults go on to sing them fun songs like "The Wheels on the Bus," "Row, Row, Row Your Boat," and "I'm a Little Teapot." And some choose to help little children learn about Jesus's love and Bible stories in songs like "Jesus Loves Me" and "He's Got the Whole World in His Hands."

As children enter preschool, parents, educators, and others use songs to teach them their ABCs, how to pick up together ("Clean Up"), how to eat healthy ("Apples and Bananas," "Hot Potato," or "Fruit Salad"), and what friendships can be ("The More We Get Together" and "The Friendship Song"). They also learn body parts ("Head, Shoulders, Knees, and Toes") and left from right ("Hokey Pokey"). In elementary school, the use of particular songs can teach children the days of the week, how to count by twos, fives, and tens, and about the different seasons ("Summer Time, Winter Time"). Songs can also teach kids about emotions ("Happy and You Know It" or "Feelings"). In fact, there are songs to cover almost any learning topic, from counting to science, and weather to manners.[1]

In addition to teaching many different concepts, songs are also frequently used to boost moods or provide motivation during exercise. Songs have been used to advocate for change globally, such as "We Are the World" and "Do They Know It's Christmas?" Both were written to raise money to feed others in countries experiencing famine.

It's easy for our children and teens to be surrounded by music—they can often access and listen to music in P.E. class, on the car radio, at home, or on their devices. A 2010 study by the Kaiser Family Foundation found that, by the age of eight, the average child spends almost an hour each day listening to music, and by the time they're sixteen, the average teen listens to three hours of music every day.[2] With music being such a prominent part of our daily lives, it's important not to overlook the influence songs can have on our children as they grow older and move from songs about friendship ("Your friends are my friends and my friends are your friends") to songs about dating relationships.

Music Videos

Negative influences reaching youth through music reached new heights with the debut of MTV in 1981. Teens no longer had to stretch their inexperienced minds to create a picture of what the songs were telling them; now MTV acted it out for them with a mere click of the remote.

The words, tunes, and videos our youth listen to and watch are important to them and influence their thoughts, feelings, and actions. Teens often choose to imitate the behaviors and messages of actors and musicians without understanding that they may be viewing something that can negatively influence them. Meanwhile society frequently dismisses music and music videos as forms of "entertainment."

The reality is many studies have now found that the messages our children are being exposed to through music affect them, especially when combined with other media messages such as those transmitted on TV and in video games and magazines. As the authors of one report noted, "Music is well-known to connect deeply with adolescents and to influence identity development, perhaps more than any other entertainment medium."[3]

The content they're being exposed to should concern parents and other adults. In the summer of 2009, songs on the top music charts were analyzed:[4]

- Sixty-nine percent referenced sex at least once.
- Forty-six percent contained sexual lyrics.
- Forty-one percent of the songs contained profanity.
- Thirty-one percent referenced drugs or alcohol.

Music videos also contain many messages about sexual activities. The Greatschools.org website shares the following facts:[5]

- "On average, music videos contain 93 sexual situations per hour, including 11 hard-core scenes depicting behaviors like intercourse and oral sex."
- "Watching a lot of sexual content on TV and listening to sexually explicit music lyrics increase the chances that a teen will have sex at an earlier age."

Additional studies report that the more teens watch music videos, the more likely they are to engage in sexual activity and approve of premarital sex.[6]

Also, those who watch music videos experience the following influences:

- Females who watch music videos are more likely to tolerate sexual harassment.[7]
- Boys who watch these videos begin to treat women as sex objects, even becoming sexually aggressive with them.[8]
- Fifty-five percent of youth surveyed believe song lyrics affect them.[9]

In addition to the messages we receive from song lyrics and videos, the **music rhythm** can also impact us. High school junior David Merrill conducted a science fair project to learn how music affects learning.[10] His theory was that hard rock impedes learning—but he discovered much more.

Merrill had three groups of mice, two of which listened to music ten hours a day during the study. At the conclusion of the study, the control group (no music) shaved five minutes off the time it took them to go through a maze. The group listening to Mozart improved their time by eight and a half minutes, but the group listening to hard rock *increased* their maze time by twenty minutes. The hard rock group also stumbled through the maze and no longer sniffed the air to find trails.

The year before, Merrill started a similar project but kept the mice of each group in cages together. He had to end the experiment early when the mice listening to hard rock music killed each other.

Studies cited in the book *The Effects of Violent Music on Children and Adolescents* report that heavy metal music has a high rate of violent and sexual content and is known to influence teens. The author shares that compared to teens who listen to mainstream music, those who listen to heavy metal report being distant from their families and have more conflict with their parents, teachers, and school administrators. They also tend to perform lower academically and engage in risky behaviors such as drunk driving, casual sex, and drug use. The author also reports that "youth in juvenile detention were three times as likely as regular high school students to be metal fans."[11] Again, I go back to the question "Has the unacceptable become acceptable?"

Have we lowered the bar and not only accepted unhealthy, immoral behavior but also condoned it with the music we listen to and allow to influence our hearts?

Cringe-Worthy

I loved the songs I grew up listening to; they were fun and familiar, and I continued listening to them until my children were in elementary school. But I began to find myself cringing as we listened to some of the songs. While some songs, like "Mickey," "Manic Monday," "Walk Like an Egyptian," "Jump," or "Born in the U.S.A.," were mild and mostly fun, other songs, like "Jesse's Girl," made me uncomfortable.

Back when I was a teen, "Jesse's Girl" was one of my favorite songs. In the song, one boy sings about wanting his friend's girlfriend and alludes to the physical intimacy the couple share. As a shy person, yet to be asked out by a boy, I wanted to be like the girl in the song—desired by not one, but two boys.

But as a mom, I didn't want lyrics about physical relationships and desire planted in my children's thoughts, especially while they were only in elementary school. I could no longer enjoy songs like "Jack & Diane," which suggests that the couple have sex in the backseat of Jack's car. Songs that had always been acceptable to me were suddenly questionable!

Initially, I thought my kids were too young to understand the meaning conveyed in these songs. But when I asked my ten-year-old what she thought it meant or tried to explain to her that the song was conveying poor behavior (such as wanting another person's girlfriend), I was usually surprised by how much she had grasped from the song. Most of the time she didn't need my explanation; and while she may not have understood all the sexual references or actions yet, some of the messaging and emotional content were already making an impression and teaching my kids about dating relationships.

Praise-Worthy

Uncomfortable with exposing my kids to these messages, I turned the station away from songs I originally had thought were harmless, and once again, I felt ultraconservative. But I also wondered again, *Am I really sheltering them, or over time have we lowered the bar, putting too much in front of our children too soon?*

Previously a friend mentioned she felt better overall when she listened to Christian music. At the time, I tried making the change, but because I wasn't familiar with many contemporary Christian songs, it felt uncomfortable at first.

My kids and I didn't enjoy the new music as much, and since I didn't want my kids to hear some of the messaging in the secular songs, I started to leave music off in the car and at home. Then I thought about the fact that I didn't want to remove music from our lives completely and that there are indeed good songs out there. So, we made a playlist of secular songs we enjoyed with positive messages and began to play that when we wanted to listen to music.

We also gave Christian music another try. Yes, it was still unfamiliar and somewhat uncomfortable for us. But this time, I reasoned that anything new could be uncomfortable at first, so I needed to give it time to become familiar. I needed to learn the lyrics and be able to sing along to some of the songs while driving in the car.

I also made another playlist of hymns and songs I enjoyed at church. This way, I had familiar Christian music when I wanted it. Do you know what? I found that my friend was right: I discovered that listening to Christian music improved my mood. Instead of missing what I didn't have, I was content and felt at peace.

Navigating Choices

Unlike TV and movies, most music is not rated for content, so it can be more difficult for parents and teens to make wise choices about the music they select.

In an attempt to alert parents of music with content that includes strong language and/or depictions of violence, sexual activity, or substance abuse, the Parents Resource Music Center (PRMC) was formed in 1985 and asked the Recording Industry Association of America (RIAA[12]) to voluntarily create guidelines or a rating system similar to the Motion Picture Association of America's (MPAA) film-rating system.[13]

After hearings with the United States Senate Committee on Commerce, Science, and Transportation, the PRMC and RIAA reached an agreement that the latter would make parental advisory labels (PALs) available to recording artists or record labels. Unfortunately, the program is voluntary, and the RIAA parental advisory logo standards state over and over, "it is recommended, but not required."[14]

So, even if labels are available, there aren't rules requiring the labeling of albums that contain explicit material. While teens under the age of seventeen are not allowed to purchase tickets for movies with an R rating, it's up to each store to create a policy regarding music sales with PALs. Thankfully, some stores, like Walmart, have decided not to carry songs or albums labeled "explicit," resulting in some artists recording an edited version with "cleaner" lyrics.[15] Other stores may decide to carry both the explicit and the revised version, and some carry only the original version.[16]

But the biggest hurdle in protecting our kids' ears comes from how easy it is to access music and songs of all kinds. It's difficult for teens to watch an R-rated movie or purchase an adult magazine, but to listen to a song that portrays sexual relationships, drinking, or violence, all they have to do is turn on their car radio or add an app on their phone and they can hear songs with such content.

Similar to helping youth navigate the messages in television shows and movies, it's beneficial if parents and other adults listen to songs or watch music videos with the youth in their lives, then discuss the content, to help the youth determine whether what they're accessing aligns with their values. Adults can also help encourage youth to listen to music or watch videos with positive messages.

Chapter 18
Social Media and the Internet: Sometimes Helpful, Sometimes Not

When my son was in third grade, we met some of his friends at the neighborhood park. After a while, the group of boys moved from playing on the slides and playscapes to hunching over something at a nearby picnic table. When I walked over to see what they were doing, I discovered they were all hovering over one of the boys' cell phones and texting a girl from school.

It caught me by surprise. Was this appropriate? I wondered if third-grade boys became comfortable texting girls ages eight and nine for playdates would they start testing the waters regarding romantic relationships sooner than they should. Does opening the door to instant contact at a young age increase the chances of "crossing the line" later?

While what I observed was an innocent experience, it opened my mind to the possibilities of how much our children can access anywhere they go (literally). As a parent I had failed to look ahead to see what things might be approaching our family around the next bend. I decided I needed to start thinking about what I could be doing to prepare and educate my kids about the choices they would have to make in the future.

In the Palm of Their Hand

Many children today own smartphones, allowing them access to television shows, movies, music, the internet, and so much more in the palm of their hand.

A 2018 Pew Research Center study reported that 95 percent of teens ages twelve to seventeen go online, and **45 percent are online on a near-constant basis** (up from 24 percent in Pew's 2015 study).[1] The software company McAfee reports that teens are online as much as six hours per day.[2] Youth (eight- to eighteen-year-olds) spend their time online connecting on social media, playing games and/or video games, instant messaging, visiting websites, and using email.

Many of our teens may not be accessing questionable content, but a majority of teens do like to communicate with their friends through social media. At least 71 percent of thirteen- to seventeen-year-olds have more than one social media account (such as Instagram, Snapchat, Facebook, and Twitter).[3] Below are a few facts about how teens use these sites:

- Fifty-one percent of teens are likely to visit their sites at least once a day.[4]
- Worrisome is the fact that many teens make friends with people they meet online; 57 percent of teens have done so, with 29 percent making more than five new friends online, and 20 percent having met *in person*.[5]

Flirting on the Net

A study by the Pew Research Center of thirteen- to seventeen-year-olds disclosed that social media also plays a key role in starting and maintaining dating relationships. While many relationships still begin in person, teens are using social media to reach out almost as much in order to flirt, talk, or express their romantic interest in one another. Teens use the following approaches:[6]

- Fifty-five percent talk in person.
- Fifty percent "friend" the other on Facebook or another social media site.
- Forty-seven percent "like," comment on, or interact with the other person on social media.
- Forty-six percent share something funny or interesting online with the person.

An article in *Psychology Today* notes that teens start flirting online by liking or following the other person on social media. They scroll through past photos and posts, adding likes or comments (known as "deepliking").[7] The comments include emojis that convey messages, and even the word *hey* has meaning when it has extra *y*'s.[8] (For example, using three *y*'s can mean the person sending it likes the person they're reaching out to.) If interest sparks from comments and likes, the teens start sending direct messages (DMs) and may move to talking, meeting in person, or starting a relationship.

Although teens with and without dating experience may send flirtatious messages or sexy photos to someone they're interested in, teens with prior dating experience are more likely to do so.[9]

A 2018 study in *JAMA Pediatrics* found that 14.8 percent of teens have sent a sext message containing a nude or seminude image, and 27.4 percent of teens have received one.[10] Obviously some of the photos sent are being shared or forwarded to someone else, often without the consent of the person who originally sent the picture.

As for the flirtatious messages themselves, they aren't always welcome: 35 percent of teen girls and 16 percent of teen boys have "blocked or unfriended someone who was flirting in a way that made them uncomfortable."[11]

Once teens are in a dating relationship, many use social media to share how they feel about the other person publicly. They also use technology to stay connected with one another and expect to hear from each other at least once a day (85 percent), every few hours (35 percent), or hourly (11 percent). They do so through a variety of ways:[12]

- Ninety-two percent communicate via text message.
- Eighty-seven percent talk on the phone.
- Seventy-six percent use social media.
- Sixty-nine percent utilize instant or online messaging.
- Fifty-five percent use video chat.
- Forty-nine percent use messaging apps.

Social media is a significant component of a teen's life and can influence dating relationships. The student news site for Ventura (California) High School, the *Cougar Press*, shares, "30% of teens cited social media platforms as playing a substantial role in maintaining and ending their relationship."[13] While social media can be beneficial for staying connected, including emotional connection, it can also lead to jealousy, causing many to feel unsure about their relationship. It also opens the door for other conflicts, as a post, comment, or something that occurred offline may lead to an online fight. Whether posts are of the couple together or a spat, other teens comment and sometimes judge, adding to the resultant turmoil.

Social Media Risks

There are many additional social media risks that go beyond the world of dating relationships:[14]

- **Cyberbullying:** Forty-seven percent of teens have witnessed cruel online behavior, 18 percent of teens have been victims of online bullying, and 13 percent of teens have been afraid to go to school due to cyberbullying.
- **Privacy issues** (which can also include what happens with sexting).
- **Internet addiction:** Many teens stay online for hours each day.
- **Sleep deprivation:** Teens stay up late texting, chatting, or surfing social media sites. Not wanting to be left out by missing a new post, comment, or text message, teens have admitted to sleeping with their phones on their stomachs, so they'll feel the vibration and wake up.
- **Depression:** Teens can feel left out if friends post activities online to which they weren't invited. Simply seeing others' lifestyles or activities, even those of acquaintances, can make teens feel left out and bad about themselves.
- **Lower self-esteem:** Teens risk damaging their self-esteem if they post selfies for likes and feel that the

number of likes received isn't high enough, or if they compare their likes to someone else's and discover that the other person has more.

- **Lower grades:** Young people who spend more time online are often spending less time studying. Checking social media during study breaks can also result in lower grades, for the same reason.

- **Influence of risky behaviors:** Teens may try risky behaviors like smoking or drinking because they saw a picture or post of a peer doing it. They may also try risky challenges they see online, such as the salt-and-ice challenge (which burns the skin), the *Bird Box* challenge (in which participants complete tasks—including driving!—blindfolded), the milk-crate challenge (walking across precariously stacked milk crates), the outlet challenge (plugging a charger into a socket and dropping a coin in the space between to cause an electrical reaction), or the cinnamon challenge (eating a spoonful of ground cinnamon without drinking water; the cinnamon coats and dries the mouth and can result in bronchial reactions such as coughing, vomiting, and the risk of pneumonia, among other health risks).

- **Potential pedophiles or other predators** may reach out and contact them.

Risky behavior has been part of our lives since time began, and each generation has its temptations. But for today's youth, *the barrier is lower, and the stakes are higher*. As a teen, I snuck into R-rated movies and risked getting caught and facing the possible consequences. Teens back then who wanted to view pornography had to acquire adult magazines somehow, whether taking them from their dad's stash or stealing some issues from the local convenience store, at the risk of serious consequences. But today's youth can access any content they want to view from the device they hold in their hands, and with very low risk.

As with censoring TV, movies, or songs, we can't hide our children in a bubble, limiting their access to anything we consider questionable, unhealthy, or dangerous. And even if we set parental controls on their devices, restricting access to harmful content, they likely have a friend willing to share their device to access that content.

Instead of controlling and scrutinizing what's on our children's devices, we have to recognize that smartphones, iPads, and other devices open the door to a new world, and we need to talk with our children about this technology that is sometimes helpful but can also be harmful. Providing this information can help teach youth how to navigate the internet or online conversations safely, guiding them to make wise, healthy choices.

Chapter 19

Valuing Family Time over Digital Time

In college, I waitressed at a local bar/restaurant. The bar area seated about forty people, and there was a large-screen TV against the wall that was usually turned on but muted. That is, until the popular sitcom *Cheers* began. At that point, someone always asked for the TV to be turned up. Invariably, every weeknight at 10:35 p.m., the TV volume would ratchet up, and the conversations in the bar would stop. No talking was allowed as the bar full of people watched other lives in the bar on TV. If someone new came in and talked during the show, they were quickly shushed. No one even placed a drink order until the commercial breaks. How ironic that a group of people out for an evening would stop their own conversations to watch a fictional group's interactions on TV.

One day, when my children were little, that time in the bar came to mind, as it dawned on me that I was doing the same thing at home with my family. My kids loved the show *Full House*, and we often watched it in the evening before bed.

I can't even begin to calculate the countless hours we gathered together to watch another family interact on TV.

While *Full House* was a good show that often imparted a worthwhile message or sparked conversation, it made me sad to realize I was doing the same thing with my family as the people did in that college-era bar. Rather than spending precious quality time together interacting, we were watching relationships develop in the lives of a TV family.

An Ever-Shifting Stream

When it comes to our kids, it's important not only to choose appropriate media content but also to manage the time we spend watching media. And while TV, movies, YouTube videos, and so on can creep into our lives and steal precious time together, often newer technology lures us even more. With the world literally at the touch of our fingertips, it's easy to get pulled into email, social media, games, or any number of other online habits, at the expense of the people right in front of us.

Like many parents today, I grew up at a time when cell phones and the internet didn't exist. And so, I have found myself, like many others, having to navigate down an unfamiliar, ever-shifting stream.

It took much debate before my daughter received her first cell phone for Christmas during fifth grade. She had started middle school that year, and her school was released thirty minutes before the elementary school. After school, she would walk a block and a half to the elementary school her brother attended, then I would meet them both there, and we'd drive home together. My ex-husband and I started considering a cell phone for her in case anything happened.

We weren't sure she really needed one but reasoned if an emergency occurred and the technology was available, didn't it make sense to provide her with that tool? We discussed the "what-if" scenarios and eventually decided to give her a cell phone. Because she was young, we added the parental control features, limiting who she could call to ten people, mostly family, with a few select friends. We also limited the time of day she could use her phone to the hours after school until just before bedtime.

As my daughter moved into junior high, she asked for the limitations on her phone to be lifted so she could communicate with more friends. I was comfortable with how she'd used it so far and felt she was responsible, so we removed the restrictions on the number of people with whom she could talk and text.

But I soon discovered I didn't like the intrusion and negative feelings cell phones brought into our lives. I found that increasing her contacts affected our time together. Gone were the days of running errands and talking while we hung out. Instead, as I drove from point A to point B, she was texting with her friends. It wasn't the texting or even communicating with her friends that bothered me. It was the interruption of our time together. Sitting beside her as she types away makes me feel like an intruder, especially when I ask who she's texting with or what they're texting about.

And as I've watched my daughter text and then anticipate a response from a friend, I've observed her checking and rechecking her phone to see if somehow she missed the sound, lights, or vibration that would alert her to an incoming text. In today's age of instant responses, hurt feelings or feelings of insecurity can ensue if a text message or invitation isn't immediately answered. I miss the days of the landline, when there was a buffer of time as we waited until we arrived home to receive a message.

Another family-phone benefit I miss is the opportunity it could provide to answer the phone, thus greeting the person on the other end of the line and interacting, even briefly, with my children's friends as my parents had with mine. Even more disappointing is the realization that as she approaches dating age, the boys she will talk with will also have the ability to access her directly rather than call the home phone, which would have given me the opportunity to answer and interact for a minute or two.

As I began to recognize the drawbacks of digital life in my home, I instituted a technology-free rule on a family vacation to a state park in Missouri, intending our time away to be devoid of digital technology so we could enjoy each other's company. As much as I relished the thought of playing board games in the evening and keeping our devices put away during the day, giving us the opportunity to talk and connect, doing so proved much harder than I thought.

I have to admit, despite my intentions, I gave in as soon as we started the trip, justifying the use of DVD players by telling myself it would make the eleven-hour car ride to our vacation destination easier.

When we arrived at the cabin that was supposed to be internet- and cable-free, I discovered both had been installed. I gave in to my children's pleas for TV the next morning and allowed them to watch a show while I made breakfast. I rationalized the decision by telling myself we were getting plenty of family together time during the day, so this time would be okay. Then I found myself breaking my own new technology-free rule as well, since it was easier to use the map on my phone to get to the state park than try to figure out on my own how to get there on unfamiliar roads.

While we didn't play board games together as I'd hoped, we still limited technology at times and had fun kayaking, fishing, and hiking together. So, although I gave in on the technology-free rules part of the time, we did connect as a family more than we would have at home.

Our Kids Need Connection, Balance—and Us

During my struggle with giving in on the technology, I had an "aha!" moment and learned I need to be more diligent in creating family time. Whether we're away on vacation or spending time together at home, that experience made me realize I have to resist the urge to give in to TV requests and instead insist on family time or game night. By allowing TV or cell phones, I'm not helping anyone; instead, I'm letting my kids also take the easy way out and decreasing our valuable and important time together. I also need to teach my kids that media is not the be-all and end-all. There is so much more that's important and on which we need to focus.

As a parent, I need to help my kids establish healthy habits during leisure time, like exercise and outdoor activity. It's also important for their development that I dedicate a technology-free day each week and/or designate hours that are off-limits to technology each day, such as family mealtime and while doing homework.

This thought isn't new. Since smartphones and tablets started being introduced into our lives, I know setting limits and house rules has crossed the minds of and been done by countless parents (including you, undoubtedly!). But often, we come up against societal influence with the argument "kids want to spend time with their friends, not with their parents." And in today's world, that means texting and using social media sites on their phones.

While it is a natural progression for teens to pull away from family and build their own identities, the reality is that children need bonds with their parents just as much through their teenage years as they do at any other stage of their development. In fact, experts agree **kids need more time with their parents during their teen years!**[1]

As our teens grow up, they encounter new situations and experiences daily. They need us to talk with them, helping them learn how to make decisions and develop values of their own so that when they're spending time with their peers, they're able to make wise choices and positively influence others, rather than make risky decisions because they don't stop to think about the consequences or because "everyone else is doing it."

Children of all ages need a safe adult person to listen to their thoughts, feelings, and fears, helping them navigate friendships and choices while preparing them to be wise, independent, thoughtful adults. They need quality time, and reassurance from their parents during these years is critical to their development. And here's why: **Teens connected with their families have better self-esteem, are more confident, and are less likely to engage in risky behavior.**[2]

When working to instill time to connect with my family, once we move past the initial resistance and start another activity—perhaps walking the dog, having family game night, or just cleaning up the kitchen after dinner together—we enjoy each other's company. We might not always have deep conversations while doing these activities, but we're connecting. We're having fun together. We're building relationships so the talks can happen.

Chapter 20

The Beauty in Being Still

One afternoon as I mowed the yard, I realized how much I relish being outside doing chores. I've always enjoyed the excuse just to be outside. But beyond being outside, doing chores *technology-free* allows me to *hear* the outside—the birds chirping, the neighbor kids playing, and at times peaceful silence. It allows me the opportunity to *see* and *appreciate* God's creation: flowers blooming or leaves falling, birds flying, or a bee pollinating a flower.

As a child I'd sit outside just to watch a worm crawl. As a teen I would lie on the trampoline and watch the clouds drift in the sky. And as a college student I'd play on the swings in the park with my roommate, the two of us alternating between talking to each other and just feeling the breeze on our faces. It's rarer for me to find and relish those quiet times now. Often when there is a moment of downtime, I fill it with email or checking Facebook.

Thankfully one of the Focus on the Family podcasts taught me how addictive technology can be, and it reminded me we need to spend time being "unplugged."[1] Since I listened to that podcast, the need to be disconnected has continued to pop up in my thoughts, and one day it made me think of running—technology-free!

For as long as I can remember, I've enjoyed running and walking outside. Whether I go for a jog outdoors on a pleasant afternoon with a light breeze or a run in the rain, it makes me feel like a kid again. I always feel better after a run, often returning from a thirty-minute jog feeling relaxed and invigorated at the same time.

Before I started running in my teen years, I delighted in riding my bike on the streets of my neighborhood. Back and forth, up and down the blocks I would travel, meandering through my neighborhood for hours at a time. Sometimes I noticed something new about a nearby house or said hi to a neighbor, but most of the time, I was just lost in my own world. I enjoyed being outside and feeling the light touch of the breeze against my skin.

Then in high school, I began to run, not for exercise, but as a release. If I was frustrated with a friend, something that happened at school, or (more often than not) a fight with my parents or boyfriend, I would bound out of the house and run hard and fast, pounding out my frustration on the pavement. Eventually, my frustration would begin to dissipate, and I would slow down, alternating between walking and jogging as I sorted my problem and feelings. I would keep going until I couldn't run anymore.

Sometimes, even after I finished running, I wouldn't feel like going back inside my home right away. So, I'd sit on the trunk of the car in the driveway, lean against the back window, and just watch the stars.

After college and as I began to work full-time, I would go to the gym and work out on the stairclimber or walk on the treadmill to stay in shape. Often, I found myself thinking through things that needed to be done at work. Then at some point I developed the habit of not leaving the gym until I was no longer thinking about work.

I continued to run once I got married and had kids because it provided a way to stay in shape and relax. But my style of running changed. Somewhere along the way, I started listening to music while I ran. Often the songs would stir up a memory in me, and I would let my thoughts be dictated by the song that came on rather than let my mind wander.

Then, when I got divorced and found myself a single parent with two small kids, I put a treadmill in the garage so I could exercise at home, often while my kids were sleeping. I found that it was hard to run on it in the garage—I only had the same three walls to look at, endlessly! So, I added a TV as a way to distract myself while I ran. While it relieved the monotony of running in my garage, I didn't realize at the time what I had lost.

Thankfully I started cycling and then running with the Leukemia & Lymphoma Society's Team In Training program. It's too dangerous to cycle outside with earphones (it's not particularly safe when running either), so I adjusted to exercising without music and discovered I liked enjoying the outdoors without the distraction of music. It was peaceful.

I also found that my mind began to wander, and as I rode, different thoughts would pop up. I would think through situations with my family or come up with a solution to something I hadn't even been thinking about when I'd left the house. I returned from the rides renewed and rejuvenated.

Unplugging

Realizing the benefits of being unplugged, I started trying to apply these new habits to other areas of my life. One of the things Bill Hybels shares in the video I mentioned in the introduction (*The Power of a Whisper: Hearing God, Having the Guts to Respond*) is that he regularly leaves the car radio off to talk and listen to God while driving. After hearing this, I started trying to leave the radio off in the car. At first, the silence felt odd, just like it did when I changed from listening to secular tunes to Christian music (chapter 17). But after giving it a try, I discovered sometimes it was a nice way to unwind.

Occasionally my kids have gotten in the car when I've had the radio off, and sometimes they'll ask me to turn on the radio; but other times we'll continue to ride without it. Now and then, when the music is on, they've even surprised me by asking me to turn it off. Sometimes we all need silence to decompress from our busy lives.

But how often do we or our kids take even a few minutes to relax or breathe deeply and just let our thoughts roll?

In his article "Growing Up Digital, Wired for Distraction," Matt Richtel shares a quote from a high school senior that summarizes the digital change in our lives: "I know I can read a book, but then I'm up and checking Facebook," he says, adding: "Facebook is amazing because it feels like you're doing something and you're not doing anything. It's the absence of doing something, but you feel gratified anyway." He concludes, "My attention span is getting worse."[2]

We've allowed ourselves and our children to avoid boredom. **But boredom is healthy!** Our brains need downtime; being unplugged is vital to our overall well-being and health, especially for kids and teens whose brains are still developing.

When we're plugged in—whether it's TV, music, video games, the internet, instant messaging, or texting with friends—our brains aren't able to relax and process all that we've learned or been exposed to that day. Our brains also weren't designed for multitasking. As much as we're taught that multitasking is a positive attribute in school and at work, we're actually less productive and produce lower-quality work when we multitask. Kids who are allowed to text, IM, or use social media while doing homework regularly get lower grades.

The following study gives just one example of how multitasking lowers productivity:

> Students taking a general psychology course were asked to read on a computer a 3,828-word passage. One group used instant messaging before they started reading, another group used instant messaging while they were reading, and a third group read without instant messaging. After subtracting the time spent instant messaging from the reading times, the group that used instant messaging while they read took between 22 and 59 percent longer to read the passage than students in the other two groups.[3]

The effect of media doesn't only pertain to disruptions while studying but also after finishing homework. Another study found that boys who were allowed to play an hour of video games *after* homework slept less soundly and showed a decline in retention of what they had studied.[4]

> We need downtime when we're awake to sleep better at night.

What we and our kids need is *downtime*. And downtime is different from sleep.

Downtime Replenishes

In recent years, scientists have discovered what is known as *brain default mode* or *default network*, which occurs when people are awake but have downtime just to think. Studies have found that sections of the brain become more active during periods of downtime or daydreaming, which allows the brain to process information, reinforce learning, regulate our emotions, solve problems, and even assess our morals.[5] In a *Scientific American* article, Ferris Jabr states:

> Downtime replenishes the brain's stores of attention and motivation, encourages productivity and creativity, and is essential to both achieve our highest levels of performance and simply form stable memories in everyday life. A wandering mind unsticks us in time so that we can learn

from the past and plan for the future. Moments of respite may even be necessary to keep one's moral compass in working order and maintain a sense of self.[6]

Downtime doesn't have to consist of just sitting around. Our minds can wander when we do easy tasks as well—like vacuuming, dusting, or raking leaves. So yes, it's true: chores are good for your kids! (As long as they aren't listening to music while doing these chores.)

The Indigo Learning blog shares the following:

> Scientists who research "unconscious thought" have found that activities that distract the conscious mind without taxing the brain seem to give people greater insight into complex problems. In a study of students who were asked to determine which car would be the best purchase, for instance, the group that spent their decision-making time solving an unrelated puzzle made better choices than the group that deliberated over the information for four minutes.[7]

Downtime is something we can all make time for. Whether you're closing your eyes to engage in deep breathing for a few minutes, taking a quick nap, exercising outside (somewhere other than in a busy, distracting urban setting, that is), or dedicating time to meditation or prayer, these actions are beneficial to your brain. Downtime of any length is valuable, providing our brains with the default mode we need to function well.

Once I learned this, I started to recognize one reason my kids become so talkative at bedtime. Almost as soon as they get into bed, the questions start to spill out. Sometimes I'm frustrated by this; after all, they've had the entire afternoon or evening to worry about a test, tell me about something they need for school, or talk about something they're concerned about. But I've realized that earlier in the day they're often too busy for their minds to think about these things! It's not until they're quieter that the thoughts can pop up and discussions start to unfold. As maturing kids and teens, our youth sometimes need help to process some of the information from the day.

These days I look forward to assisting my children in sorting through some of their questions and thoughts, even if it's at bedtime. The necessity of downtime has also prompted me to think about how and where we can add mental downtime into our days. When my daughter was little, she'd often share thoughts and feelings with me while we worked on an art project together. As she gets older, I search for other projects we can do to provide downtime and the opportunity to talk through things if needed. But I also need to teach my children to *seek* downtime and build it into their lives as they get older.

PART THREE

HEALING

Chapter 21
Meeting God

When I was in my early forties, two experiences happened that began to reshape my life. First, I suffered a concussion, and it took seeing three doctors before one finally diagnosed the concussion.

The last doctor told me I just needed "time to heal" and should continue with my daily routine. So, for the next six weeks, I worked and took care of my kids (ages six and ten) but continued to struggle with nausea, overwhelming fatigue, and short-term memory loss. I tried to push through, but sometimes I was in tears from exhaustion at the end of the day.

Since I wasn't getting better, I went back to see the doctor. He placed me on medical leave from work to give my brain time to heal. In addition to prescribing time off to rest, the doctor also recommended I not watch TV, read, or use the computer.

The first weekend of medical leave, I was at home alone, with absolutely nothing to do. Feeling lonely and isolated, I wandered out into the backyard. The last six weeks had been scary, and now instead of the doctor reassuring me I was getting better, he had placed me on medical leave! It worried me that the doctor was concerned, and I was anxious about what would happen next if I didn't heal during the prescribed time off.

Racked with worry, I tried to reassure myself with conventional thoughts:

- I had my health. (*Well, not really. . . .*)
- I had a good job. (*But what if I wasn't able to return to it at the end of my medical leave?*)
- I had a nice house. (*Would I be able to continue making my mortgage payments and covering our other living expenses if my health didn't improve and I couldn't return to work?*)

It felt like everything was slipping away . . . until I realized **the only "thing" we can be assured of is God**. While growing up in my church I'd learned *God is always there for us. God will never change.* Everything I relied on could slip away—but not God.

The explosive thoughts that I might lose everything combined with the recognition that only God is always there for me made me feel completely exposed to God. The poor decisions I'd made over the years lay in front of me, and I couldn't hide myself behind distractions like television and work. My entire being was filled with remorse. Alone with God now, I felt utterly unworthy.

The shame I carried brought me to tears. I wanted God's love and forgiveness, but I'd done so many bad things (especially premarital sex) that I couldn't bring myself to ask my heavenly Father to forgive me. And so, just as Adam and Eve hid after eating the apple, I went inside the house to "hide" from God and the sins I'd committed. I wanted to draw near to God but was ashamed to do so after so many years of pulling away.

Over the next few days, these thoughts and the resultant struggle I had with approaching God kept bouncing through my mind. Then, within a week or two, the second event occurred.

A few weeks before the concussion, my kids and I had started attending church when I heard the message I mentioned in the introduction to this book. While I was listening to that DVD in Sunday school, I heard God saying, "This doesn't change who you are. I still love you," and I realized that included me. God was reaching out to me! The years of guilt and shame began to wash away.

When God spoke to me through the message, His love wrapped around me. I was significantly comforted and began to accept His unconditional love. But since I had pulled away from God for so many years, I also felt lost. I didn't understand *how* I was supposed to live as a Christian or what I was supposed to *do* daily. One evening, a good friend since college was at my house for dinner. He attended church and Bible Study Fellowship (BSF) regularly and had even volunteered with his church's youth group. After dinner, we were sitting on the couch talking, and I asked him those questions.

He asked for a Bible, and I gave him the one I kept in my nightstand. He flipped through it and read Galatians 5:22–23 to me:

> *But the fruit of the Spirit is love, joy, peace, forbearance, kindness, goodness, faithfulness, gentleness and self-control.*

A light turned on for me. ***The Bible had directions for me!*** Sure, I had learned Bible verses in Sunday school when I was young, but I didn't remember any of them. And although at one point I knew a few Bible verses, I had never *read* the Bible.

A few times throughout my life, I had tried. But in those instances, I found the words and messaging hard to understand—and in some places scary—so I'd put the Bible away before I had read even one whole book of the Bible.

But now I wanted to know more, and I knew that the Bible, God's Word, would guide me. After my friend left, I picked up the Bible and read the verses preceding Galatians 5:22. This particular section was equally meaningful to me:

> *The acts of the flesh are obvious: sexual immorality, impurity and debauchery; idolatry*

and witchcraft; hatred, discord, jealousy, fits of
rage, selfish ambition, dissensions, factions and
envy; drunkenness, orgies and the like.
(Galatians 5:19–21)

I had experienced some of those things, and they didn't feel good. Sure, when I was at a party with my friends in college, it seemed fun to get drunk together. The next day we even bonded as we commiserated about our hangovers. But while I felt like part of the group, there was also a part of me that felt empty and experienced regret. At the time, I didn't know why I felt this way, but I didn't like it.

Up to this point, I didn't know much beyond this: God loved me, and His Son, Jesus Christ, died on the cross. In fact, as a child, I frequently misunderstood the Bible's teachings, and I also thought God was the master puppeteer, and we were the puppets. I didn't like the idea of being controlled, and rebelliously I pushed away from His love.

But as I read these Bible verses and then all of the fifth chapter of Galatians, at this critical point in my life, things began to make sense.

God doesn't want to keep us from having fun; He wants to protect us from a lifestyle that hurts us.

> Our heavenly Father wants to guide us toward a better life here on earth, a life filled with joy, peace, and contentment, and eventually eternal life with Him.

As I began to understand the significance of the messages in the Bible and God's love, I became hungry for more. My thirst for what else God had to tell me was unquenchable, and for the first time in my life, I began to read the Bible to seek and know the Lord God Almighty.

Growth and Knowledge

As I started reading the Bible, I also worked through Beth Moore's Bible study *Living Beyond Yourself: Exploring the Fruit of the Spirit*. It further helped me understand God's divine love.

We use the word *love* to describe how we feel about many things, from "I love my husband/wife/children/parents/siblings" to "I love chocolate!" Because we use the word *love* so broadly, it can be hard to understand just how deeply God loves each of us.

As I studied God's love, I learned that the New Testament was originally written in Aramaic and Greek. In the Greek language, there are *four* words to describe different types of love. Knowing the different meanings helped me understand God's deep love:[1]

- **Storge** refers most often to *familial love*, or the love we have for our children and other family members.
- **Philia** refers to *friendship*. This type of love involves giving and taking. It includes loyalty to friends, family, and community and requires virtue, equality, and familiarity.
- **Eros** refers to *physical love*. It can also be used to convey feelings that are stronger than a *philia* love and thus refers to feelings between a husband and wife.
- **Agape** is the most significant type of love. *Agape* was used by early Christians to express the unconditional love God has for us. It is described throughout the New Testament as *sacrificial* and *spiritual* love. This love is selfless; it gives and expects nothing in return. The apostle Paul describes *agape* best:

> *Love is patient, love is kind. It does not envy, it does not boast, it is not proud. It does not dishonor others, it is not self-seeking, it is not easily angered, it keeps no record of wrongs. Love does not delight in evil but rejoices with the truth. It always protects, always trusts, always hopes, always perseveres. Love never fails.*
>
> (1 Corinthians 13:4–8)

As I continued to read and study, I also began to grasp that, although understanding and relying on His Word is essential, God also wants a relationship with us. That can be confusing. God is more significant than any person we've ever known, and yet God can feel abstract and distant. How do we have a relationship with God?

As I pondered this question, I thought about how I felt about and interacted with the people in my life. And that helped clarify some things. For example, if I were married, wouldn't I want to talk and spend time with my husband every day? Yes! Because I cared about him, I'd like to know how he was doing and what thoughts were on his mind. I'd want to celebrate his joys and help him through difficult times.

And as a parent, don't I want to spend time with my children each day? Yes! Whether talking with them during breakfast, helping them with homework after school, having dinner together, or tucking them into bed at night, I find any moment I can share with them a blessing and a joy.

And while I may not see or talk to my friends as regularly as my family, it's important to me to make time to visit with them, support them, and share in their lives because I care about them. So, as I thought about the people in my life and the time I share with them, I began to realize how our heavenly Father feels about us. God loves us more than we can know, and He wants a relationship with us. He wants us to share our joys with Him, and He wants to comfort us when we're troubled—

each and every day, each and every moment.

Reaching Out His Hand

As I began to comprehend God's deep love for me, I also realized that He'd tried to reach out many times in my life and call me back to Him. But I wasn't paying attention.

After I dated Brock, I still prayed to God and occasionally felt Him comforting me. But out of shame over some of my life choices, I kept my distance. Now, though, when I look back over my life, **I'm in awe of all the times the Lord God tried to reach me before I finally looked up from my pain and recognized His voice**.

Just as a shepherd gently guides the sheep away from harmful situations, watches over them while they sleep, and leads them to food and water, God is the ultimate Good Shepherd. He is always seeking us and calling us home to a life with Him.

Chapter 22
God's Everlasting Love

As I continued to read the Bible and reflect on its messages, I began to learn additional insights and truths.

> *The Lord appeared to him from far away. I have loved you with an everlasting love; therefore I have continued my faithfulness to you.*
>
> (Jeremiah 31:3 ESV)

> *Give thanks to the God of heaven*
> *for his steadfast love endures forever.*
>
> (Psalm 136:26 ESV)

Not only does God care for us now, but He loves each of us so much that **He wants us to accept His love and spend all eternity with Him.**

Reading numerous times throughout the Bible that God's desire is to love and be with us always was *powerful*.

I wanted to live my life for God and follow what I was learning in the Bible, but I was worried I would forget what I was learning or how to apply it to my life going forward. Partly this was because I had learned so very much through reading about how Jesus lived His life. I wished I could talk to Him, learn more from Him, and have Him guide me.

I was so relieved to learn that although Jesus is no longer here in person, we can pray to Him. And I was incredibly grateful that Jesus left the Holy Spirit to guide and help us. I'd always heard about the Father, Son, and Holy Spirit, but I'd never fully grasped the significance. Before Jesus left this world, He gave us a promise that He was sending the Holy Spirit to help us until His return, telling the disciples:

> *But the Helper, the Holy Spirit, whom the*
> *Father will send in my name, he will teach you*
> *all things and bring to your remembrance all*
> *that I have said to you.*
>
> (John 14:26 ESV)

But God didn't just send the Holy Spirit to live with us in this world. God goes a step further and seals the Holy Spirit in our hearts when we choose to believe:

> *In him you also, when you heard the word of*
> *truth, the gospel of your salvation, and believed in*
> *him, were sealed with the promised Holy Spirit.*
>
> (Ephesians 1:13 ESV)

*Now it is God who makes both us and you stand
firm in Christ. He anointed us, set his seal of
ownership on us, and put his Spirit in our hearts
as a deposit, guaranteeing what is to come.*

(2 Corinthians 1:21–22)

As I continued to read the Bible, I was also reminded how important it is to keep reading because its stories and teachings continue to help guide us.

Your word is a lamp for my feet, a light on my path.

(Psalm 119:105)

God's Love Forgives

To read so many examples of God's love and how much He cares for each of us, regardless of anything we've done, was astounding. I'd love to say my life changed overnight as a result of this knowledge, but despite reading of God's love over and over again, I still struggled with guilt for the poor choices I'd made as a teen and young adult. I tried to let go of my past but continued to feel remorse for poor choices I'd made.

Forgiving myself and letting go of my past was difficult. Long-embedded shame and guilt were holding me back from accepting God's forgiveness. Regret over my choices and forgiveness were two teachings I tried to understand and accept as I read the Bible.

One day as I was praying, God placed two Bible passages on my heart:

> *The LORD is compassionate and gracious,*
>   *slow to anger, abounding in love.*
> *He will not always accuse,*
>   *nor will he harbor his anger forever;*
> *he does not treat us as our sins deserve*
>   *or repay us according to our iniquities.*
> *For as high as the heavens are above the earth,*
>   *so great is his love for those who fear him;*
> *as far as the east is from the west,*
>   *so far has he removed our transgressions from us.*
>   (Psalm 103:8–12)

"As far as the east is from the west." That's significant! **He removed my sins from me more than I could ever hope or imagine.**

The other passage was:

> *Brothers and sisters, I do not consider myself*
> *yet to have taken hold of it. But one thing I do:*
> *Forgetting what is behind and straining toward*

what is ahead, I press on toward the goal to
win the prize for which God has called me
heavenward in Christ Jesus.

(Philippians 3:13–14)

When the Apostle Paul wrote the words above, he was telling the Philippians how much he wanted a life with Jesus Christ. Paul, formerly known as Saul, also had a past that he was not proud of. Before becoming a Christian, Saul had persecuted and killed Christians. One day, when he was on his way to imprison more Christians, a bright light flashed before him and Saul fell to the ground. Jesus spoke to him, asking Saul why he was persecuting Him. When Saul stood up, he was blind.

The men with Saul led him to a house in Damascus, where Saul prayed for three days. God called a disciple, Ananias, to go to Saul and lay his hands on him so his sight would be restored. Although Ananias was afraid Saul would arrest him when he did so, he listened to God and went to where Saul was staying. Ananias laid his hands on Saul's eyes and proclaimed God's plan, and Saul's sight was restored. Then Saul chose to be baptized as a follower of Christ.[1]

Through God's love, Saul was made new and became Paul, a faithful disciple proclaiming the gospel and converting thousands to Christianity throughout parts of Asia and Europe. If God could forgive Saul for killing and transform his heart, surely God could also forgive and change me.

I knew I too had to stop looking backward. I had to stop dwelling on past mistakes and turn my thoughts to the present and future.

With this revelation, I finally was able to forgive myself, fully accepting God's love, grace, and mercy. Gratefully I accepted God's love, received Him into my heart, and rededicated my life to Him.

Chapter 23
Believing Jesus

One morning the Bible verse below grabbed my attention (emphasis added):

> *For this is the will of my Father, that* **everyone who looks on the Son and BELIEVES in him should have eternal life,** *and I will raise him up on the last day.*
>
> (John 6:40 ESV)

When I was growing up, at Easter my family and I often watched a reenactment of the story of Easter—Jesus's crucifixion and resurrection. I knew the story. But this verse made me stop and wonder *if I believed* the story was real. For although I was grateful for Jesus's teachings and examples when He walked with the disciples, did I believe He was more than just a devout man? Did I really know and believe that Jesus Christ was God in human form and born to die so my sins could be forgiven?

I looked back to the previous chapter in John and read:

Very truly I tell you, whoever hears my word
and believes him who sent me has eternal life
and will not be judged but has crossed over
from death to life.

(John 5:24)

Then I asked myself, *Do I believe God raised Jesus from the dead so that I may have eternal life?*

I lay in bed as I grasped the meaning in these verses and pondered the questions, thinking through everything I had read and learned up to this point. Previously, I'd never thought it was significant that *four* disciples or close acquaintances of disciples had written accounts of Jesus's life, death, and resurrection, but now I understand it was for our benefit. It wasn't just one person telling us about Jesus—there were *four* separate reports from among the many eyewitnesses and their contemporaries.

As I walked through what I had learned about Jesus, I concluded that I *did believe* Jesus was a live person, not just a character in a story I'd heard at Easter. But He's not just a person—I believe Jesus is the Son of God, God incarnate. He was born to die so my sins could be forgiven, and God raised Jesus from the dead so that I may have eternal life. **I accepted Jesus into my heart as my Lord and Savior.**

Chapter 24
Moving Forward

So now I knew that, above all else, God was my heavenly Father who loved me unconditionally, so much that He wanted to spend all eternity with me. I had accepted Jesus Christ as my Lord and Savior. I prayed that the Holy Spirit was inside my heart to guide me. I had learned and believed the most important truths, and out of awe and respect for these miraculous gifts, I pondered more than ever, *How do I live my life going forward?*

I decided my first steps were to keep reading the Bible, praying, reflecting, and learning to let the Holy Spirit guide me. As I read the Bible, this thought was reinforced by these verses:

> *Hear, O Israel: The LORD our God, the LORD*
> *is one. Love the LORD your God with all your*
> *heart and with all your soul and with all your*
> *strength. These commandments that I give you*
> *today are to be on your hearts. Impress them on*
> *your children. Talk about them when you sit at*
> *home and when you walk along the road, when*

you lie down and when you get up. Tie them as
symbols on your hands and bind them on your
foreheads. Write them on the doorframes of
your houses and on your gates.

(Deuteronomy 6:4–9)

The information and commandments in the Bible were important—so important we were to talk about them frequently, do things to remember them, put them in front of ourselves, and teach them to our children. I had never lived a life like that, and this thought was powerful.

I also began to wonder, *If I had known these truths and turned to the Bible for wisdom as a youth, could it have helped me make better choices?* When I came upon the Scripture below, it answered my question (emphasis added):

**How can a young person stay on the path of
purity?**
By living according to your word.
I seek you with all my heart;
do not let me stray from your commands.
I have hidden your word in my heart
that I might not sin against you.
Praise be to you, Lord;
teach me your decrees.
With my lips I recount

all the laws that come from your mouth.
I rejoice in following your statutes
 as one rejoices in great riches.
I meditate on your precepts
 and consider your ways.
I delight in your decrees;
 I will not neglect your word.

(Psalm 119:9–16)

As I continued to ask God how to move forward, I also began to ask how I could help young people. And I felt led to share my story and my experience with others in hopes it could help another teen avoid the type of abuse and shame I endured as a youth, and inform a family so they could help their developing youths.

As a result, my life began to change. First thing each morning I spent time reading the Bible, praying, and journaling. On the Saturdays my kids were with their dad, I began to write. After a few hours, I'd go on a run and sort through the section I was working on and ask the Holy Spirit to lead me in what to write. Then I'd come home and write some more and continue to pray.

It wasn't easy. Often, I would pace in my kitchen as I wrestled with how to share something I'd researched or with trying to see where Jesus was guiding me to go next in this book.

My life was "quiet," and it looked different from many of the examples of how women live that we see on TV (on shows like *Friends*, *Fuller House*, *Grey's Anatomy*, or *Desperate Housewives*). So, sometimes I felt as if I was supposed to go out and date. Sometimes old habits, like watching TV in the afternoon or scrolling social media, pulled at me.

But when I stopped to reflect, I knew I didn't want to do any of the other things. I was content, and I knew I was doing what I was meant to do. I relied on the teaching in the Bible to help guide me to follow Jesus, including this verse:

> *Do not conform to the pattern of this world, but be transformed by the renewing of your mind. Then you will be able to test and approve what God's will is—his good, pleasing and perfect will.*
>
> (Romans 12:2)

Rock-Solid Foundation

As I wrote, researched, and learned, I sought answers to the question "What can we instill in our kids to give them the foundation they need to stay away from risky behaviors?" I looked to conventional ideas such as self-confidence and self-esteem. But as I thought through those concepts, I realized friendships can change, parents or siblings can become sick, and academics or sports can get harder for all of us across time and circumstances. So, essentially almost anything we base our identity on can be affected—*except our identity as children of God.*

God is the only one who will always be with us. Not only does God want what is best for us, but He loves us unconditionally. In fact, He loves each of us so much that He wants to be with us for all eternity. The concept I had started to grasp in my backyard after the concussion became more concrete. **A foundation built on God's love provides the rock-solid foundation each of us needs to guide us through life.**

To develop this rock-solid foundation, we need to spend time reading the Bible and to seek Almighty God with our entire being; otherwise it's easy to misconstrue His message and get swayed, even pulled away, by this world. Many studies have found that Christians today make the same choices as non-Christians, such as getting divorced, having premarital sex, and experiencing teen pregnancies at the same rate as non-Christians.[1] But studies also show that **a Christian who reads the Bible at least four times a week leads a different life.**[2]

Around the time I was rediscovering the teachings in the Bible, I listened to a speaker from Focus on the Family share a story about a teenager whose mother was an alcoholic. The teen knew he didn't want to follow in her footsteps, but he also knew there were days ahead when he might be tempted. So, he prepared himself by reading the Bible, finding and memorizing several Bible verses he could lean on in times of temptation. The speaker shared that while the boy was at a celebration with a group of friends, they encouraged him to drink. Each time they approached the teen, he responded with one of the Bible verses he had memorized. By relying on God's Word, he was able to resist temptation successfully.

> *Wine is a mocker and beer a brawler; whoever*
> *is led astray by them is not wise.*
>
> (Proverbs 20:1)

Like the young man in the example above, I had to choose whether I would live a life of the flesh— following the harmful messages and examples set by the world we live in, a life that can hurt us and pull us away from God—or if I was going to live a Spirit-filled life, following Jesus while seeking a joyful, peace-filled life with God by protecting my eyes, ears, mind, and ultimately heart.

Following Jesus

The following contrasting verses have really resonated with me as I've worked to turn away from the things of this world and follow Him.

> *She does not ponder the path of life; her ways wander, and she does not know it.*
>
> (Proverbs 5:6 ESV)

> *Ponder the path of your feet; then all your ways will be sure.*
>
> (Proverbs 4:26 ESV)

This message was reinforced for me on a family trip when we visited a prospective university for my daughter. Our family drove into town from one side, and after the tour, we headed back to stay at a friend's house in Dallas via a different route. Despite the fact that I had never been in this town before, I assumed I knew which way to turn once we got to the right highway. So, without even checking a road sign, I got on Interstate 75, expecting to see the suburbs of Dallas in about twenty minutes. Instead, the roadside stayed barren of buildings or houses, and the next thing I knew we saw a sign that said, "Welcome to Oklahoma."

What?! How did we get to Oklahoma? I wondered. I started looking for a road sign. The next one I saw showed we were on I-75 *North* when we needed to be on I-75 *South*. I took the next exit, did a U-turn, and got us headed in the right direction. Thankfully everyone found humor in my mistake, and it sparked a great conversation with my kids about the wisdom in the verses from Proverbs.

While the choice I made that day was a small one, often the choices in life are bigger. Too many times, because I haven't paused even for a few minutes to consider my options and all the possible outcomes, I've made a choice I regretted. Whether the choice we make is big or small, it always has an impact.

Now, I try to make choices that follow Jesus.

Chapter 25
Making the Changes

Following the path God has laid out for me reminds me of the street where I live. It's a U-shaped street that intersects the main road at two different points. The intersection closest to my house has a blind curve, and frequently, drivers who want to turn left there get halfway onto the main road before seeing a car heading toward them from the right.

At the intersection on the opposite end of the street, not only are both lanes of oncoming traffic completely visible to the driver merging onto the main lane, but the other drivers also have stop signs, making it a much safer intersection. The first intersection is hazardous to use, and yet most of us living on my street choose to get on the main road from this point simply because it's closer and saves us a few seconds. Although it's risky, it's easy and convenient. But one neighbor chooses to go out of her way to the other intersection because it's safer, reminding me of the Scripture

Enter through the narrow gate. For wide is
the gate and broad is the road that leads to

destruction, and many enter through it. But
small is the gate and narrow the road that leads
to life, and only a few find it.

(Matthew 7:13–14)

Many of the distractions that face us today are similar to the choice between those two intersections. We choose them because they're easy or familiar. So, at the end of the day, it's easy—both for our children and for us—to turn on the TV and veg out. Maybe it feels overwhelming to learn about the technology age our kids are living in and how to keep them safe, so we give in to letting them have the devices, often with unrestricted access. Maybe it's uncomfortable or feels like a battle to have these conversations with our kids. Or we watch movies or listen to music because it's what we've always watched or listened to. Other times, we make decisions because "everyone else is doing it (or has it)," ignoring the risks and the longer but safer route.

Many of the ideas and changes I've made in my life happened as God led me to research and write this book. Whether it was listening to different music or watching new television shows and movies, the change was hard and uncomfortable at first. As I've sought His direction for my life, He's quietly whispered thoughts and ideas into my heart, showing me how to make these changes.

It can take time to adjust and change old habits, but if we work at it, if we're prayerful about it, and if we keep trying, we'll get there. And as with most things in life, once we reach the other side, we'll be amazed at what we discover when we reach out to God for the strength and courage to persevere.

> *You make known to me the path of life; you will fill me with joy in your presence, with eternal pleasures at your right hand.*
>
> (Psalm 16:11)

My Mental U-Turn

I was reading the book *The Daniel Plan*, which is about leading a healthier life. The writers assert that faith is the first element of a healthy life. In the chapter about faith, one of the authors, pastor Rick Warren, writes:

> The biblical word for personal change is *repentance* . . . It [repentance] comes from the Greek word *metanoia*, which means to change your perspective, think in a different way, make a mental U-turn. Of course, if you change your mind, your behavior will follow, but repentance starts in the mind, not in actions.[1]

Interestingly, there's a Bible verse I've always liked, and it wasn't until I read *The Daniel Plan* that I began to realize I had always misunderstood its first line. The verse is:

> This is what the Sovereign LORD,
> the Holy One of Israel, says:
> "In repentance and rest is your salvation,
> in quietness and trust is your strength,
> but you would have none of it."
>
> (Isaiah 30:15)

Previously I focused on "in quietness and trust is your strength," appreciating the wisdom from it that I needed quiet time with God, and that my strength comes from that quiet time and trust in Him. Now I had a new understanding of repentance in the verse due to reading *The Daniel Plan*, and the minister at my church mentioned *metanoia* just a few weeks later!

During that sermon, the minister explained that **repentance means to learn a new way to live**. He also reminded us that since sin constantly tries to tempt us in this world, we need to practice ongoing repentance and continue reading Scripture so we can stay on God's path and grow in Jesus's character.

I believe we can do this on both a personal and a societal level.

Turning the Current Tide

Studies in recent years have found that although many Americans believe there is a moral decline in our nation and that reading the Bible would help us, only 45 percent of American adults attend church on a monthly basis, and only 28 percent read the Bible several times each week.[2] But if we choose to read Scripture consistently and follow Jesus, we're going to be different.

While our society has strayed from biblical teachings over time, resulting in declining morals and values, it doesn't have to be this way. There have been times when we've made cultural changes that have positively impacted our lives to give us hope for the future. So, change is quite possible.

One example of a cultural change we've made is with tobacco. Smoking was a socially acceptable custom and desired habit for most of the twentieth century. When studies began to emerge about the health hazards of smoking, the tobacco industry tried to hide that information.

A forty-year-long battle ensued, with brave individuals advocating for the truth about the detrimental side effects of tobacco while uncovering the layers of deception created by the tobacco industry.[3] But change did occur, and people today are healthier for it.

> So, just as diligent, thoughtful people have changed the social norms with regard to smoking and other destructive behaviors, we can turn the tide on the negative messages that surround us today.

Still, sometimes I wonder why the world is the way it is, and why we have to struggle against negative messages and outcomes. When those questions come to mind, I find assurance in the following verses:

> *I do not ask that you take them out of the world, but that you keep them from the evil one. They are not of the world, just as I am not of the world. Sanctify them in the truth; your word is truth. As you sent me into the world, so I have sent them into the world.*
>
> (John 17:15–18 ESV)

*If then you have been raised with Christ, seek
the things that are above, where Christ is,
seated at the right hand of God. Set your minds
on things that are above, not on things that are
on earth.*

(Colossians 3:1–4 ESV)

I hope you find assurance in them as well.

Epilogue
Following God: Answered Prayers

Getting involved to help youth continued to be something I thought about. I learned that after faith, family, and school connections, the biggest protective factor for a youth is to be involved in their community. I felt called to work with youth, to talk with them about healthy relationships and ways for them to get involved in their community. But how?

I started researching programs that taught high school students about abusive dating relationships. I knew I was being led to volunteer in a school setting, and I was drawn to volunteering either in the school district of my high school alma mater or at the one my kids were attending. At the time, I worked in an office about twenty minutes from both of these districts. The volunteer work would have to be on my lunch break, so I wondered how I could volunteer when just getting to one of the schools and back would take up most of a lunch hour.

I began to pray, "God, if you want me to volunteer in the schools, my job needs to allow me to work from home." And so, on my drive to work, throughout the day, when I made dinner, and when I tucked my kids into bed at night, that prayer, along with "Show me what you want me to do," was always in my mind and heart.

I didn't know how it would happen. At the time, I'd worked for the same organization for ten years; and although I was able to work from home a few hours each week, positions based at home simply didn't exist. And then, after a year of praying, a new position opened—one that I was excited about. At the end of the conversation with my prospective new boss, she concluded with "Oh, and this position is remote. You'll have to work from home."

God answered the prayer He'd placed in my heart a year earlier!

I moved into the new position and began working from home. I continued praying about what I should do, asking God, "What does the youth program look like?"

I heard that the youth director at our church volunteered at another high school, so I arranged to meet with him. When we met, he gave me some materials from a program called "Core Essential Values." The goal of this program was to help kids instill positive character traits in themselves and their peers. I felt like I'd been given a huge gift. I left the meeting at the church overwhelmed at the commitment it would involve, but also overjoyed to have some tools to begin the club and talk with teens about love, joy, kindness, goodness, self-control, and other positive character traits.

Now I needed to reach out to the schools. But work was busy. One chaotic day I lamented to God, "If I can't make a phone call to meet with the school, how am I going to get away during the work/school day to meet with youth?" In response to my prayer, I felt the answer: "Use the time spent on social media to make phone calls instead."

At that time I occasionally took a break from my workday to scroll on social media, with my intended two- or three-minute break often turning into ten or fifteen minutes. So, the very next time I felt the urge to take a short break, I called the school. The appointments I needed were scheduled within the week!

The school quickly approved the idea of forming a school club about positive character traits, and twelve junior high students were nominated to join. We sent them invitations to the first meeting. It was exciting, and I knew I was following Jesus and listening to the Holy Spirit guide me, but as I parked my car at the junior high, I broke out in a cold sweat.

Questions raced through my mind. *What am I doing? I don't know anything about working with junior high students.* So, I did the only thing I could: as I walked toward the building, then toward the classroom where we would meet during lunch, I prayed. "God, I don't have any experience doing this. I don't know how to engage teenagers. Please show me what to do and let the words that come out of my mouth be yours." He led me that week and every week after that.

The first club started in January 2014. It became known as PIE Club (for Positively Influencing Everyone). The following year PIE Club moved to the high school when the students transitioned there, and a new club was started at the intermediate school. The goal was for the students to be part of the club from their fifth through twelfth grades, learning about each positive trait three times during those years.

But we needed to do more than just talk about the traits; we needed ways to put them into action. So, the third year we started an annual Christmas food giveaway. PIE Club obtains food for families in need, and on the day of the giveaway the teens sort and package the food and carry it to the families' cars. I love watching the teens grow and teach younger students, and especially their hearts for helping others. My other favorite part of this day is when we pause the activities to say a prayer before beginning to give the food away.

All answered prayers.

Resources

National Domestic Violence Hotline:
1-800-799-7233 or TTY 1-800-787-3224 or thehotline.org.

Love Is Respect (National Teen Dating Abuse Hotline):
1-866-331-9474, text LOVEIS to 22522. Live chat is also available on the organization's website, loveisrespect.org.

Rape, Abuse & Incest National Network (RAINN) Hotline:
800-656-HOPE (4673). Live chat is also available on the organization's website, rainn.org.

A list of additional resources for victims of teen dating violence can be found at Youth.gov.

Many states also offer local resources for teen dating violence and sexual assault/date rape.

National Suicide Prevention Lifeline:
1-800-273-8255 or three-digit dialing code 988. Live chat is also available on the organization's website, suicidepreventionlifeline.org.

Notes

Introduction

[1] "Teen Dating Violence Statistics," Domestic Violence Services, Inc. (website), accessed June 12, 2022, https://www.dvs-or.org/teen -dating-violence-statistics/; 33% of an estimated 425 females.

Chapter 1 – Beginning to Date

[1] Sarah Sorensen, "Adolescent Romantic Relationships," ACT for Youth Center of Excellence Research Facts and Findings, Dibble Institute, July 2007, https://dibbleinstitute.org/Documents/reasearch_facts _romantic_0707.pdf.

[2] Liz Claiborne, Inc., "Teen Relationship Abuse Survey (Conducted March 2006)," Break the Cycle (website), accessed 2011, https://www .breakthecycle.org/sites/default/files/pdf/survey-lina-2006.pdf.

[3] Amanda Lenhart, Monica Anderson, and Aaron Smith, "Teens, Technology and Romantic Relationships," Pew Research Center, October 1, 2015, https://www.pewresearch.org/internet/2015/10/01 /teens-technology-and-romantic-relationships/; Robin Hattersley-Gray, "Dating Abuse Statistics Everyone Should Know," *Campus Safety*, December 12, 2012, https://www.campussafetymagazine.com /safety/dating-abuse-statistics/.

Chapter 2 – Emotional Abuse

[1] Celeste Inman, M.Ed., LPC-S, RPT-S, email message to author, October 3, 2020.

[2] Jennifer Huizen, "What Is Verbal Abuse?" *Medical News Today*, December 18, 2019, https://www.medicalnewstoday.com/articles /327346#types-of-verbal-abuse.

[3] Breckan E. Winters, "How Can Advocates Raise Awareness about Emotional Abuse for Teen Dating Violence Awareness and Prevention Month (TDVAM)?" VAWnet (website), February 3, 2020, https://vawnet.org/material/how-can-advocates-raise-awareness -about-emotional-abuse-teen-dating-violence-awareness-and.

[4] National Center for Mental Health Promotion and Youth Violence Prevention, "Teen Dating Violence: Prevention, Identification and Intervention," National Center Brief, November 2011, 8, http:// www.promoteprevent.org/sites/www.promoteprevent.org/files /resources/Teen%20Dating_0.pdf; "Recognizing and Intervening in Emotionally Abusive Teenage Relationships," Social Work License Map (website), March 2, 2021, https://socialworklicensemap.com /blog/emotional-abuse-teen-relationships/.

[5] Ramin Setoodeh, "Tracey Gold on Her Eating Disorder TV Series 'Starving Secrets,'" *Daily Beast*, November 8, 2011, http://www .thedailybeast.com/articles/2011/11/08/tracey-gold-on-her-eating -disorder-tv-series-starving-secrets.html.

[6] Liz Claiborne, Inc., "Tween and Teen Dating Violence and Abuse Study," Scribd, February 2008, https://www.scribd.com/document /384242013/violencia-en-adolescentes.

[7] The lists in this section were compiled from several sources. Please see:

Winters, "How Can Advocates Raise Awareness"; Ann Pietrangelo and Crystal Raypole, "How to Recognize the Signs of Mental and Emotional Abuse," Healthline, updated January 28, 2022, https://www.healthline.com/health/signs-of-mental-abuse; Karly Hemp, "An Adolescent Dating Abuse Prevention Curriculum," SlidePlayer, accessed November 7, 2021, https://slideplayer.com/slide/1588413/; Melinda Smith and Jeanne Segal, "Domestic Violence and Abuse," HelpGuide (website), updated January 2021, https://www.helpguide.org/articles/abuse/domestic-violence-and-abuse.htm; "Is Emotional Abuse More Harmful Than Physical Abuse?" MHS (Mental Health Services website), May 14, 2021, https://www.mhs-dbt.com/blog/is-emotional-abuse-more-harmful-than-physical-abuse/; Natasha Tracy, "Effects of Emotional Abuse on Adults," HealthyPlace (website), December 17, 2021, http://www.healthyplace.com/abuse/emotional-psychological-abuse/effects-of-emotional-abuse-on-adults/; "Emotional Abuse," Thisiswar.com (website), accessed 2011, http://www.thisisawar.com/AbuseEmotional.htm (site discontinued); "Characteristics of Healthy & Unhealthy Relationships," Youth.gov, accessed November 7, 2021, https://youth.gov/youth-topics/teen-dating-violence/characteristics.

Chapter 3 – Sexual Coercion

[1] Liz Claiborne, Inc., "Tween and Teen Dating Violence and Abuse Study," Scribd, February 2008, https://www.scribd.com/document/384242013/violencia-en-adolescentes.

[2] "Trends in the Prevalence of Sexual Behaviors and HIV Testing National YBRS 1991–2019," Centers for Disease Control and Prevention, updated August 20, 2020, https://www.cdc.gov/healthyyouth/data/yrbs/factsheets/2019_sexual_trend_yrbs.htm.

[3] Brian P. Dunleavy, "CDC: 40% of Teens Are Sexually Active," UPI,

May 6, 2020, https://www.upi.com/Health_News/2020/05/06/CDC-40-of-US-teens-are-sexually-active/8811588709258/.

[4] Casey E. Copen, Anjani Chandra, and Gladys Martinez, "Prevalence and Timing of Oral Sex with Opposite-Sex Partners among Females and Males Aged 15–24 Years: United States, 2007–2010," Centers for Disease Control and Prevention, August 16, 2021, 10, https://www.cdc.gov/nchs/data/nhsr/nhsr056.pdf.

[5] Collin Allen, "Peer Pressure and Teen Sex," *Psychology Today*, May 1, 2003, https://www.psychologytoday.com/us/articles/200305/peer-pressure-and-teen-sex.

[6] Silvi Saxena, "Peer Pressure: Types, Examples & How to Respond," Choosing Therapy (website), December 9, 2020, https://www.choosingtherapy.com/peer-pressure/.

[7] Michele Ybrra and Kimberly Mitchell, "Prevalence Rates of Male and Female Sexual Violence Perpetrators in a National Sample of Adolescents," *JAMA Pediatrics* 167, no. 12 (December 2013): 1125–34, https://doi.org/10.1001/jamapediatrics.2013.2629.

[8] Liz Claiborne, Inc., "Teen Relationship Abuse Survey," Break the Cycle (website), 2006, accessed 2011, https://www.breakthecycle.org/sites/default/files/pdf/survey-lina-2006.pdf.

[9] Liz Claiborne, Inc., "Teen Relationship Abuse Survey."

[10] "Emerging Issues Facing Tweens and Teens," MesaAZ.gov, accessed October 30, 2021, https://www.mesaaz.gov/Home/ShowDocument?id=7922.

[11] Laura Kann, Tim McManus, William A. Harris, Shari L. Shanklin, Katherine H. Flint, Joseph Hawkins, Barbara Queen, et al., "Youth Risk Behavior Surveillance—United States, 2015," Centers for Disease

Control and Prevention, *Morbidity and Mortality Weekly Report* 65, no. 6 (June 10, 2016): 10–11, 71, https://www.cdc.gov/healthyyouth /data/yrbs/pdf/2015/ss6506_updated.pdf.

[12] Miranda Hitti, "Teen Sex May Take Emotional Toll," WebMD, February 6, 2007, https://www.webmd.com/sex-relationships/news /20070206/teen-sex-may-take-emotional-toll.

[13] Kirk Johnson, Lauren Noyes, and Robert Rector, "Sexually Active Teens Are More Likely to Be Depressed and to Attempt Suicide," Heritage Foundation (website), June 3, 2003, https://www.heritage .org/education/report/sexually-active-teenagers-are-more-likely-be -depressed-and-attempt-suicide.

[14] "Sexual Risk Behaviors Can Lead to HIV, STDs and Teen Pregnancy," Centers for Disease Control and Prevention, updated June 14, 2021, https://www.cdc.gov/healthyyouth/sexualbehaviors/index.htm.

[15] "Sexually Transmitted Diseases—Adolescents and Young Adults," Centers for Disease Control and Prevention, updated April 8, 2021, https://www.cdc.gov/std/life-stages-populations/adolescents -youngadults.htm.

[16] Adapted from various Focus on the Family broadcast episodes. Used with permission; "3 Reasons You Should Want Your Child to Wait to Have Sex," iMOM, accessed June 12, 2022, https://www.imom.com/3 -reasons-should-want-child-wait-have-sex/.

[17] "Words for Saying No," B4uDecide, accessed June 12, 2022, https:// b4udecide.ie/your-decision/saying-no-to-sex/words-for-saying-no/.

[18] "Talking with Your Teens about Sex: Going Beyond 'the Talk,'" Centers for Disease Control and Prevention, November 2014, https:// www.cdc.gov/healthyyouth/protective/factsheets/talking_teens.htm.

Chapter 4 – Denial

[1] "The 4 Stages of Battered Women's Syndrome," Laws.com, December 29, 2019, http://marriage.laws.com/domestic-violence /battered-person-syndrome/stages-of-battered-womens-syndrome /stages-of-battered-womans-syndrome#sthash.cOu1w89u.dpuf.

[2] "Is Your Teen in an Abusive Relationship?" Familydoctor.org, April 17, 2020, https://familydoctor.org/teen-abusive-relationship/; Callie Rennison and Sara Welchans, "Intimate Partner Violence," U.S. Department of Justice, May 2000, https://bjs.ojp.gov/content/pub/pdf /ipv.pdf; Sharon Smith, Xinjian Zhang, Kathleen Basile, Melissa Merrick, Jing Wang, Marcie-jo Kresnow, and Jieru Chen, "The National Intimate Partner and Sexual Violence Survey: 2015 Data Brief–Updated Release," Centers for Disease Control and Prevention, November 2018, 10, https://www.cdc.gov/violenceprevention/pdf /2015data-brief508.pdf.

[3] "Prevalence of Teen Dating Violence," Youth.gov, accessed November 13, 2021, https://youth.gov/youth-topics/prevalence-teen -dating-violence.

[4] "Fact Sheet Intimate Partner Violence & Teen Dating Violence," Boston Public Health Commission, accessed November 21, 2021, https://www.bphc.org/whatwedo/violence-prevention/start-strong /Documents/Intimate_Teen_Dating.pdf.

[5] Amrutha Ramaswamy, Usha Ranji, and Alina Salganicoff, "Intimate Partner Violence (IPV) Screening and Counseling Services in Clinical Settings," Kaiser Family Foundation, December 2, 2019, https://www .kff.org/womens-health-policy/issue-brief/intimate-partner-violence -ipv-screening-and-counseling-services-in-clinical-settings/.

6 "Teen Dating Violence," J. Flowers Health Institute, accessed April 16, 2022, https://jflowershealth.com/teen-dating-violence/.

7 "H.R. 3297 (113th): Teen Dating Violence Education Act of 2013," GovTrack, October 16, 2013, https://www.govtrack.us/congress /bills/113/hr3297/text.

8 "Teen Dating Abuse Fact Sheet," New York State, Office for the Prevention of Domestic Violence, accessed July 5, 2021, https://www .ny.gov/sites/default/files/atoms/files/teen-fact-sheet.pdf.

9 Antoinette Davis, "Interpersonal and Physical Dating Violence among Teens," National Council on Crime and Delinquency, September 2008, 3, https://www.evidentchange.org/sites/default /files/publication_pdf/focus-dating-violence.pdf.

10 Jamie DePolo, "Understanding Breast Cancer, Risk" BreastCancer .org, last updated July 14, 2022, https://www.breastcancer.org /symptoms/understand_bc/risk/understanding.

Chapter 5 – Components of Physical Abuse

1 Lundy Bancroft, *Why Does He DO That? Inside the Minds of Angry and Controlling Men* (New York: Berkley Books, 2003), 319.

2 Meg Meeker, *Boys Should Be Boys: 7 Secrets to Raising Healthy Sons* (Washington, DC: Regnery Publishing, 2022), 58–59.

3 Bancroft, *Why Does He DO That?*, 329.

4 "Risk and Protective Factors for Perpetration," Centers for Disease Control and Prevention, updated November 2, 2021, https://www.cdc.gov/violenceprevention/intimatepartnerviolence /riskprotectivefactors.html.

[5] Department of Health and Human Services, *Youth Violence: A Report of the Surgeon General* (Rockville, MD: Office of the Surgeon General (US), 2001), chapter 4, https://www.ncbi.nlm.nih.gov/books/NBK44294/.

Chapter 6 – Reasons for Keeping Quiet and Staying

[1] "Teen Talk Outreach and Education Program," Beacon of Hope Crisis Center, accessed November 13, 2021, https://beaconofhopeindy.org/teen-talk-outreach-and-education-program.html.

[2] "Why Teens Stay in Abusive Relationships," Rape and Abuse Crisis Service, accessed November 13, 2021, https://cdn.website.thryv.com/bf0307f4aafd4b268a96851c5b7aff09/DESKTOP/pdf/imagea0f8.pdf?i=2548555.pdf&fn=; "Why People Stay: It's Not Always as Easy as Walking Away," National Domestic Violence Hotline, accessed November 13, 2021, https://www.thehotline.org/support-others/why-people-stay-in-an-abusive-relationship/.

Chapter 7 – Physical Violence

[1] Avanti Adhia, Mary A. Kernic, David Hemenway, Monica Vavilala, and Frederick Rivara, "Intimate Partner Homicide of Adolescents," *JAMA Pediatrics* 173, no. 6 (April 15, 2019): 571–77, https://doi:10.1001/jamapediatrics.2019.0621.

Chapter 8 – Despair and Depression

[1] "Fast Facts: Preventing Teen Dating Violence," Centers for Disease Control and Prevention, updated February 28, 2022, https://www.cdc.gov/violenceprevention/intimatepartnerviolence

/teendatingviolence/fastfact.html; Michele Cacardi and Ashley Bujalski, "When Love Hurts: How to Avoid Teen Dating Violence," Anxiety.org, July 18, 2016, https://www.anxiety.org/teen-dating-violence-how-to-avoid-tdv-and-anxiety.

[2] Melinda Smith, Lawrence Robinson, and Jeanne Segal, "Depression Symptoms and Warning Signs," HelpGuide, updated October 2021, https://www.helpguide.org/articles/depression/depression-symptoms-and-warning-signs.htm.

Chapter 9 – Sexual Assault

[1] "Date and Acquaintance Rape," Susan B. Anthony Project, accessed June 19, 2022, https://sbaproject.org/just-for-teens/date-and-acquaintance-rape/.

[2] California Coalition Against Sexual Assault (CALCASA), *2008 Report: Research on Rape and Violence* (Sacramento, CA: CALCASA, 2008), 18, http://www.calcasa.org/wp-content/uploads/2009/09/CALCASA_Stat_2008.pdf.

[3] Laura Kann, Tim McManus, William Harris, Shari Shanklin, Katherine Flint, Joseph Hawkins, Barbara Queen, Richard Lowry, Emily O'Malley Olsen, David Chyen, et al., "Youth Risk Behavior Surveillance–United States, 2015," *MMWR Surveillance Summaries* 65, no. SS-6 (2016): Table 21, https://www.cdc.gov/mmwr/volumes/65/ss/ss6506a1.htm.

[4] "Date and Acquaintance Rape." See also Holly Baxter, "The Maryville Rape Case: Social Media Hurt Daisy Coleman—Now It Is Helping Her," *New Statesman*, October 19, 2013, https://www.newstatesman.com/science-tech/2013/10/maryville-rape-case-social-media-hurt-daisy-coleman-now-it-helping-her.

[5] "Date and Acquaintance Rape."

Chapter 10 – Breakup Risks and Dangers

[1] "Eighteen Months after Leaving Domestic Violence Is Still the Most Dangerous Time," Battered Women's Support Services (BWSS), accessed June 20, 2022, https://www.bwss.org/eighteen-months-after-leaving-domestic-violence-is-still-the-most-dangerous-time/; "Barriers to Leaving an Abusive Relationship," Center for Relationship Abuse Awareness, accessed June 20, 2022, http://stoprelationshipabuse.org/educated/barriers-to-leaving-an-abusive-relationship/.

[2] Sarah LeTrent, "When a Friend Won't Walk Away from Abuse," CNN, January 10, 2013, https://www.cnn.com/2013/01/10/living/friend-domestic-abuse.

Chapter 11 – Trying to Move On

[1] Deinera Exner-Cortens, John Eckenrode, and Emily Rothman, "Longitudinal Associations between Teen Dating Violence Victimization and Adverse Health Outcomes," *Pediatrics* 131, no. 1 (2013): 71–78, https://doi.org/10.1542/peds.2012-1029; Tara Culp-Ressler, "STUDY: Teen Dating Violence Leaves a Lasting Impact on Adult Well-Being," ThinkProgress.org, December 10, 2012, https://archive.thinkprogress.org/study-teen-dating-violence-leaves-a-lasting-impact-on-adult-well-being-b2c8f09a6574/.

[2] Henrik Edberg, "How to Break Out of a Victim Mentality: 7 Powerful Tips," Positivity Blog, updated August 25, 2020, http://www.positivityblog.com/index.php/2009/10/09/how-to-break-out-of-a-victim-mentality-7-powerful-tips/.

³ Natalie Boyd, "How Seligman's Learned Helplessness Theory Applies to Human Depression and Stress," Study.com, updated August 25, 2021, https://study.com/academy/lesson/how-seligmans -learned-helplessness-theory-applies-to-human-depression-and -stress.html#lesson.

Chapter 13 – Warning Signs of Unhealthy Relationships

¹ The lists in this section are compiled from several sources. Please see:

"Healthy, Unhealthy and Abusive Relationships," University of Colorado Boulder, Office of Victim Assistance, accessed July 3, 2022, https://www.colorado.edu/ova/healthy-unhealthy-and-abusive -relationships; Kendra Anderson, "How to Tell If You're in an Unhealthy or Abusive Relationship," Mindsoother Therapy Center, June 10, 2018, https://www.mindsoother.com/blog/how-to-tell -if-youre-in-an-unhealthy-or-abusive-relationship; Break the Cycle (website), accessed 2012, https://breakthecycle.org/; "Signs of Teen Dating Violence," Teen DV Month (website), accessed October 23, 2021, https://www.teendvmonth.org/resources/signs -teen-dating-violence/; "Early Warning Signs of Dating Violence," RAINN (website), February 6, 2017, https://www.rainn.org/news /early-warning-signs-dating-violence; "Teen Dating Violence," Harbor House (website), accessed October 23, 2021, https:// www.harborhousedv.org/resources/teen-dating-violence/#safety -alert; "What Does Teen Dating Abuse Look Like?" New York State (website), accessed November 20, 2021, https://www.ny.gov

/teen-dating-violence-awareness-and-prevention/what-does
-teen-dating-abuse-look; "Is Your Teen in an Abusive Relationship?"
Familydoctor.org, updated April 17, 2020, https://familydoctor
.org/teen-abusive-relationship/; Holly W. Cummings,
"What You Can Do If You Think Your Teen Is in an Abusive
Relationship," American College of Obstetricians and
Gynecologists, October 2020, https://www.acog.org/womens
-health/experts-and-stories/the-latest/what-you-can-do-if-you
-think-your-teen-is-in-an-abusive-relationship; "Parents | Help
Your Son or Daughter," Reachout, October 31, 2018, https://www
.reachoutwny.org/parents/; Lisa Davis, "10 Signs Your Teen Is in
an Unhealthy Relationship," Family Resources (website), January
4, 2019, https://familyresourcesinc.org/2019/01/signs-teen
-unhealthy-relationship/; Kate Taylor, "10 Signs Your Friend Is in
an Abusive Relationship and Might Need Your Help," Safe Horizon,
January 2018, https://www.safehorizon.org/safe-horizon-in-the
-news/abusive-relationship-signs/; "What Is Dating Violence?"
Violence Prevention Works!, accessed October 23, 2021, https://
www.violencepreventionworks.org/public/recognizing_dating
_violence.page; "Signs to Look for in an Abusive Personality,"
City of Knoxville (website), accessed June 24, 2022, https://
www.knoxvilletn.gov/government/city_departments_offices
/police_department/criminal_investigations/special_crimes
_unit/domestic_violence_help/signs_to_look_for_in_an
_abusive_personality; "Am I in a Healthy Relationship?"
KidsHealth.org, February 2017, https://kidshealth.org/en/teens
/healthy-relationship.html.

Chapter 14 – What to Say, What to Do: Helping a Teen If You Suspect Abuse

[1] "For Parents: What Every Parent Needs to Know," Texas Advocacy Project, accessed November 20, 2021, https://www.texasadvocacy project.org/power-based-abuse/what-you-need-know/parents.

[2] Lundy Bancroft, *Why Does He DO That? Inside the Minds of Angry and Controlling Men* (New York: Berkley Books, 2003), 62–63, 371.

[3] "Safety Planning," loveisrespect.org, accessed 2012, https://www .loveisrespect.org/get-help/safety-planning (site discontinued).

[4] "Why Do People Stay in Abusive Relationships?" loveisrespect.org, accessed 2012, https://www.loveisrespect.org/is-this-abuse/why-do -people-stay-in-abusive-relationships (site discontinued).

[5] Brian Alexander, "Girls Commit Dating Violence as Often as Boys, Study Shows," NBCNews.com, July 31, 2013, https://www.nbcnews .com/healthmain/girls-commit-dating-violence-often-boys-studies -show-6c10809607. Italics are mine.

Chapter 15 – Too Much Too Soon: Media Influence

[1] CMP Automotive Ltd., "2014 Buick LaCrosse–Dance," 2014, YouTube video, 01:55, https://www.youtube.com/watch?v=XXbxa5GC9Zw.

[2] "US TV Ad Spend and Influence," Marketing Charts, December 23, 2013, https://www.marketingcharts.com/television-22524.

[3] "TV Ads Reach—and Influence—College Students," Marketing Charts, August 29, 2012, https://www.marketingcharts.com/television -23088.

4 Rachel Siegel, "Tweens, Teens and Screens: The Average Time Kids Spend Watching Online Videos Has Doubled in 4 Years," *Washington Post*, October 29, 2019, https://www.washingtonpost.com/technology/2019/10/29/survey-average-time-young-people-spend-watching-videos-mostly-youtube-has-doubled-since/.

5 Victoria Rideout, Alanna Peebles, Supreet Mann, and Michael B. Robb, *The Common Sense Census: Media Use by Tweens and Teens, 2021* (San Francisco: Common Sense, 2022), 3, https://www.commonsensemedia.org/sites/default/files/research/report/8-18-census-integrated-report-final-web_0.pdf.

6 Victoria Rideout, Ulla G. Foehr, and Donald F. Roberts, *Generation M²: Media in the Lives of 8- to 18-Year-Olds* (Menlo Park, CA: Henry J. Kaiser Family Foundation, 2010), 4, https://www.kff.org/wp-content/uploads/2013/04/8010.pdf.

7 David Hill, Nuheen Ameenuddin, Yolanda (Linda) Reid Chassiakos, Corinn Cross, Jenny Radesky, Jeffrey Hutchinson, Alanna Levine, Rhea Boyd, Robert Mendelson, Megan Moreno, et al., "Media Use in School-Aged Children and Adolescents," *Pediatrics* 138, no. 5 (2016): e20162592, https://doi.org/10.1542/peds.2016-2592.

8 Craig Anderson, Leonard Berkowitz, Edward Donnerstein, L. Rowell Huesmann, James D. Johnson, Daniel Linz, Neil M. Malamuth, and Ellen Wartella, "The Influence of Media Violence on Youth," *Psychological Science in the Public Interest* 4, no. 3 (December 2003): 103, https://journals.sagepub.com/doi/pdf/10.1111/j.1529-1006.2003.pspi_1433.x.

9 Paul David Tripp, *Age of Opportunity: A Biblical Guide to Parenting Teens* (Phillipsburg, NJ: P&R Publishing, 2001), 115.

Chapter 16 – Television and the Movies: What They're Showing Our Kids

[1] *Sex on TV* 4 (Menlo Park, CA: Henry J. Kaiser Family Foundation, 2005), 2–5, https://www.kff.org/wp-content/uploads/2013/01/sex -on-tv-4-executive-summary.pdf. Italics are mine.

[2] Candie's Foundation and *Seventeen* magazine, "Let's Talk Teens, Sexuality and Media," University of Washington, accessed August 21, 2021, http://depts.washington.edu/sexmedia/printouts/handout -surveyresults.pdf.

[3] Jeffrey A. Gottfried, Sarah E. Vaala, Amy Bleakley, Michael Hennessy, and Amy Jordan, "Does the Effect of Exposure to TV Sex on Adolescent Sexual Behavior Vary by Genre?" *Communication Research* 40, no. 1 (February 1, 2013), https://www.ncbi.nlm.nih.gov /pmc/articles/PMC3812950/.

[4] Todd Huffman, "Sexuality in Modern Media: How Is It Affecting Our Children?" unpublished letter, February 2008, https://www .mckenzie-pediatrics.com/shop/images/MediaSexuality.pdf.

[5] *Sex on TV* 4, 7.

[6] James L. Baughman, *Same Time, Same Station* (Baltimore: Johns Hopkins University Press, 2007), 1, 28–53; James L. Baughman, "Television Comes to America 1947–1957," University of Wisconsin, Madison, accessed 2011, http://www.lib.niu.edu/1993/ihy930341.html (site discontinued).

[7] John Redford, "Impact of Television: A Natural Experiment in Three Communities," TVEVOLUTION (blog), January 1995, https:// tvevolution.wordpress.com/impact-of-television-on-children-by -tannis-macbeth-williams/.

[8] Tannis MacBeth Williams, *The Impact of Television: A Natural Experiment in Three Communities* (Cambridge, MA: Academic Press, 1986), 319–25, 372–75, 396–97, 399, 401–402.

[9] Council on Communications and Media, "Media Violence," Pediatrics 124, no. 5 (November 1, 2009): 1495–1503, https://doi.org /10.1542/peds.2009-2146.

[10] Lawrence Reed, "Youth Violence and the Media," Mackinac Center for Public Policy, December 1, 2006, https://www.mackinac.org/8091.

[11] Craig Anderson, Leonard Berkowitz, Edward Donnerstein, L. Rowell Huesmann, James D. Johnson, Daniel Linz, Neil M. Malamuth, and Ellen Wartella, "The Influence of Media Violence on Youth," *Psychological Science in the Public Interest* 4, no. 3 (December 2003): 103, https://journals.sagepub.com/doi/pdf/10 .1111/j.1529-1006.2003.pspi_1433.x.

[12] Donald E. Cook, Clarice Kestenbaum, L. Michael Honaker, and E. Ratcliffe Anderson, "Joint Statement on the Impact of Entertainment Violence on Children," American Academy of Pediatrics, July 26, 2000, http://www.craiganderson.org/wp-content/uploads/caa/VGVpolicy Docs/00AAP%20-%20Joint%20Statement.pdf.

[13] Council on Communications and Media, "Media Violence," *Pediatrics* 124, no. 5 (November 2009): 1495–503, https://doi.org /10.1542/peds.2009-2146; Anderson, Berkowitz, Donnerstein, et al., "The Influence of Media Violence on Youth."

[14] Anderson, Berkowitz, Donnerstein, et al., "The Influence of Media Violence on Youth," 81.

[15] Adapted from Focus on the Family broadcast episode. Used with permission.

Chapter 17 – What Did That Song Just Say? In a World of Unlimited Song Choice

[1] Songs for Teaching (website), accessed August 21, 2021, https://www.songsforteaching.com/index.html.

[2] Victoria Rideout, Ulla G. Foehr, and Donald F. Roberts, *Generation M²: Media in the Lives of 8- to 18-Year-Olds* (Menlo Park, CA: Henry J. Kaiser Family Foundation, 2010), 5, https://www.kff.org/wp-content/uploads/2013/04/8010.pdf.

[3] Tara Parker-Pope, "Under the Influence of . . . Music?" Well (blog), *New York Times*, February 5, 2008, https://well.blogs.nytimes.com/2008/02/05/under-the-influence-ofmusic/?searchResultPosition=1.

[4] Sarah Knoploh, "Sex, Drugs, Rock-N-Roll . . . and More Sex," MRC Culture, August 19, 2009, http://archive2.mrc.org/node/28576.

[5] GreatShools staff, "Sexual Behavior: What Teens Learn from Media," GreatSchools, September 25, 2014, https://www.greatschools.org/gk/articles/sexual-behavior-teens-learn-from-media/.

[6] Yuanyuan Zhang, Laura Miller, and Kristen Harrison, "The Relationship between Exposure to Sexual Music Videos and Young Adults' Sexual Attitudes," *Journal of Broadcasting and Electronic Media* 52, no. 3 (August 2008): 368–86, https://www.researchgate.net/publication/233122934_The_Relationship_Between_Exposure_to_Sexual_Music_Videos_and_Young_Adults'_Sexual_Attitudes.

[7] Zhang, Miller, and Harrison, "The Relationship," 370.

[8] "Music Videos Promote Sexuality and Profanity and Teens Love It," Child Refuge (website), accessed July 2011, http://childrefuge.org/music/music-videos-promote-sexuality-and-profanity-and-teens-love-it.html (site discontinued).

9 "Do Bad Lyrics Really Affect Teenagers?" YouthMinistry.com, accessed August 22, 2021, https://youthministry.com/do-bad-lyrics -really-affect-teenagers/.

10 Dorothy Lockhart Lawrence, "Using Music in the Classroom," PastPapers (website), accessed October 23, 2021, 4, https://pastpapers .ie/sites/default/files/Using%20Music%20in%20the%20Classroom .pdf; Lorraine Eaton, "Mozart or Rock?" *Virginia Pilot*, July 24, 1997, https://scholar.lib.vt.edu/VA-news/VA-Pilot/issues/1997/vp970724 /07240420.htm.

11 Donald F. Roberts, Peter G. Christenson, and Douglas A. Gentile, "The Effects of Violent Music on Children and Adolescents," Research Gate, January 2003, chap. 8, 160–61, https://www.researchgate .net/publication/222094713_The_effects_of_violent_music_on _children_and_adolescents.

12 "Resources and Learning," RIAA (website), accessed August 22, 2021, https://www.riaa.com/resources-learning/parental-advisory-label/.

13 Wikipedia, s.v. "Parents Music Resource Center," updated August 1, 2022, 15:27, https://en.wikipedia.org/wiki/Parents_Music_Resource _Center; "Resources and Learning," RIAA (website), accessed August 22, 2021, https://www.riaa.com/resources-learning/parental-advisory-label/.

14 "PAL Standards," RIAA (website), October 23, 2006, https:// www.riaa.com/resources-learning/pal-standards/; "5 Surprising Facts about Parent Advisory Labels," Decades, August 28, 2017, https://www.decades.com/lists/5-surprising-facts-about-parental -advisory-labels.

15 Nekesa Mumbi Moody, "Green Day: No-Go on Wal-Mart Policy on Edited CDs," ABC News, May 21, 2009, http://abcnews.go.com /Business/story?id=7649837.

[16] Wikipedia, s.v. "Parents Music Resource Center."

Chapter 18 – Social Media and the Internet: Sometimes Helpful, Sometimes Not

[1] Monica Anderson and Jingjing Jiang, "Teens, Social Media and Technology 2018," Pew Research Center, May 31, 2018, https://www.pewresearch.org/internet/2018/05/31/teens-social-media-technology-2018/; Amanda Lenhart, "Teens, Social Media and Technology Overview 2015," Pew Research Center, April 9, 2015, https://www.pewresearch.org/internet/2015/04/09/teens-social-media-technology-2015/.

[2] "McAfee Digital Deception Study 2013: Exploring the Online Disconnect between Parents & Pre-Teens, Teens and Young Adults," Mcafee.com, accessed 2014, http://www.mcafee.com/us/resources/reports/rp-digital-deception-survey.pdf (site discontinued).

[3] Lenhart, "Teens, Social Media and Technology Overview 2015."

[4] "Social Media and Teens," American Academy of Child & Adolescent Psychiatry, updated March 2018, https://www.aacap.org/AACAP/Families_and_Youth/Facts_for_Families/FFF-Guide/Social-Media-and-Teens-100.aspx.

[5] Amanda Lenhart, "Chapter 1: Meeting, Hanging Out and Staying in Touch: The Role of Digital Technology in Teen Friendships," Pew Research Center, August 6, 2015, https://www.pewresearch.org/internet/2015/08/06/chapter-1-meeting-hanging-out-and-staying-in-touch-the-role-of-digital-technology-in-teen-friendships/.

[6] Amanda Lenhart, Monica Anderson, and Aaron Smith, "Teens, Technology and Romantic Relationships," Pew Research Center,

October 1, 2015, https://www.pewresearch.org/internet/2015/10/01/teens-technology-and-romantic-relationships/.

[7] Katherine Nguyen Williams, "Teenage Dating in the Digital Age," *Psychology Today*, February 11, 2020, https://www.psychologytoday.com/us/blog/the-modern-child/202002/teenage-dating-in-the-digital-age.

[8] "Teen Voices: Dating in the Digital Age," Pew Research Center, accessed November 7, 2021, https://www.pewresearch.org/internet/interactives/online-romance/.

[9] Lenhart, Anderson, and Smith, "Teens, Technology and Romantic Relationships."

[10] Sheri Madigan, Anh Ly, Christina L. Rash, Joris Van Ouystel, and Jeff R. Temple, "Prevalence of Multiple Forms of Sexting Behavior Among Youth: A Systematic Review and Meta-analysis," *JAMA Pediatrics* 172, no. 4 (April 2018): 327–35, doi.org/10.1001/jamapediatrics.2017.5314.

[11] Lenhart, Anderson, and Smith, "Teens, Technology and Romantic Relationships."

[12] Lenhart, Anderson, and Smith, "Teens, Technology and Romantic Relationships."

[13] Jack Schatzman, "How Does Social Media Affect Teen Relationships?" *Cougar Press*, March 11, 2019, https://thecougarpress.org/6861/features/how-does-social-media-effect-teen-relationships/.

[14] "How Social Media Affects Teens," Youth Equipped to Succeed, March 18, 2022, https://justsayyes.org/jsy-blog/how-social-media-affects-teens/; "Social Media and Teens," American Academy of Child & Adolescent Psychiatry, March 2018, https://www.aacap.org

/AACAP/Families_and_Youth/Facts_for_Families/FFF-Guide/Social
-Media-and-Teens-100.aspx; Anna Vannuccia, Emily G. Simpson, Sonja Gagnon, and Christine McCauley Ohannessian, "Social Media Use and Risky Behavior in Adolescents: A Meta-Analysis," *Journal of Adolescence* 79 (February 2020): 258–74, https://www.researchgate .net/publication/338979439_Social_media_use_and_risky _behaviors_in_adolescents_A_meta-analysis; "Teen Behavior and Experiences on Social Networking Sites," End to Cyberbullying Organization, accessed October 23, 2021, https://endcyberbullying .org/cyber-bullying-statistics/teen-behavior-and-experiences-on -social-networking-sites/.

Chapter 19 – Valuing Family Time over Digital Time

[1] Chun Bun Man, Susan M. McHale, and Ann C. Crouter, "Parent-Child Shared Time from Middle Childhood to Late Adolescent: Developmental Course and Adjustment Correlates," *Child Development*, 83, no. 6 (August 23, 2012): 2089–103, https://doi.org/10.1111/j.1467-8624.2012.01826.x.

[2] Purinda Gunasekara, "No Matter How Old They Are, They Need Their Parents," Kidspot (website), January 10, 2013, https://www .kidspot.com.au/parenting/no-matter-how-old-they-are-they-need -their-parents/news-story/77bd49ff750f81d4b05192207a32793e.

Chapter 20 – The Beauty in Being Still

[1] Adapted from Focus on the Family broadcast episode. Used with permission.

2 Matt Richtel, "Growing Up Digital, Wired for Distraction," *New York Times*, November 21, 2010, https://www.nytimes.com/2010/11/21/technology/21brain.html.

3 Maryellen Weimer, "Students Think They Can Multitask. Here's Proof They Can't," The Teaching Professor (website), September 26, 2012, https://www.teachingprofessor.com/topics/for-those-who-teach/multitasking-confronting-students-with-the-facts/.

4 Richtel, "Growing Up Digital."

5 Hallie Smith, Untitled blog post, Indigo Learning, March 27, 2014, http://indigolearning.co.za/home/the-benefits-of-downtime-why-learners-brains-need-a-break-by-hallie-smith-ma-ccc-slp/.

6 Ferris Jabr, "Why Your Brain Needs More Downtime," *Scientific American*, October 15, 2013, https://www.scientificamerican.com/article/mental-downtime/.

7 Smith, Untitled blog post.

Chapter 21 – Meeting God

1 Beth Moore, *Living Beyond Yourself: Exploring the Fruit of the Spirit* (Nashville, TN: LifeWay Press, 1998), 52–71.

Chapter 22 – God's Everlasting Love

1 See Acts 9:1–19.

Chapter 24 – Moving Forward

1 Ronald Sider, "The Scandal of the Evangelical Conscience: Why Don't Christians Live What They Preach?" ChristianityToday

.com, accessed July 4, 2022, http://www3.dbu.edu/jeanhumphreys /SocialPsych/evangelicalmind.htm.

[2] Arnie Cole and Michael Ross, *Unstuck: Your Life. God's Design. Real Change* (Bloomington, MN: Bethany House Publishers, 2012), 56.

Chapter 25 – Making the Changes

[1] Rick Warren, Daniel Amen, and Mark Hyman, *The Daniel Plan: 40 Days to a Healthier Life* (Grand Rapids, MI: Zondervan, 2013), 62.

[2] Caleb K. Bell, "Poll: Americans love the Bible but don't read it much," Religion News Service, April 4, 2013, http://www.religionnews .com/2013/04/04/poll-americans-love-the-bible-but-dont-read-it -much/; Kirk Hadawy and P. L. Marler, "Did You Really Go to Church This Week? Behind the Poll Data," Religion Online, accessed July 4, 2022, https://www.religion-online.org/article/did-you-really-go-to -church-this-week-behind-the-poll-data/; Glen Bickford, "Review: 'The American Church in Crisis' by David Olson," Bickford Mediation, accessed July 18, 2011, http://www.resolveconflictnow.net/review -the-american-church-in-crisis-by-david-olson/; American Bible Society, *The State of the Bible* 2014 (Ventura, CA: Barna Group, 2014), http://www.americanbible.org/uploads/content/state-of-the -bible-data-analysis-american-bible-society-2014.pdf.

[3] Joseph Kay, "Government Case Exposed Conspiracy of US Tobacco Giants," World Socialist Web Site, June 13, 2005, http://www.wsws.org /en/articles/2005/06/tob2-j13.html; Anne Landman, "Deadly Deception: The Tobacco Industry's Secondhand Smoke Cover Up," PRWatch, January 7, 2009, http://www.prwatch.org/news/2009/01/8115 /deadly-deception-tobacco-industrys-secondhand-smoke-cover;

Matthew Meyers, "Henry Waxman Showed America the True Face of the Tobacco Industry," Campaign for Tobacco-Free Kids, January 30, 2014, http://www.tobaccofreekids.org/press_releases/post/henry _waxman_showed_america_the_true_face_of_the_tobacco_industry.

Acknowledgments

I owe deepest gratitude to so many.

First, to my children, who listened when I shared information as I learned it and sat next to me during TV shows and movies as I pointed out the false realities—to the point that they began to be able to point them out to me or know what I was going to say before I said it. Thank you for understanding my past and never judging me for it. I am so honored to be your mom and very thankful for getting to watch you grow, explore, and learn and the years together laughing, crying, hiking, playing, talking, and so much more. You've grown into amazing young adults. I love you.

To my parents, who prayed for me without ceasing during and after the storm, who always love, support, and cheer for me.

To my sister, who is always there for me. I can't imagine life without you, and I'm so grateful for our close friendship.

To Linda, my lifelong best friend, who has shown me unconditional love and support on earth. Your grace and giving heart astound me.

To Jenna, for listening to and supporting me as I healed from my past. I'm thankful for our conversations, your steadfast support, and our friendship.

To Sylvia and Angela, thank you for being my accountability partners. I'm grateful to have you in my life, studying the Bible together, and that we shared and grew in our faith walks together.

To Teri, Nancy, Trina, Anna, Debbie, Lisa, Melanie, Sheri, and Michelle: Thank you for being with me through different parts of this journey. I'm glad we walk through life together, and I am so grateful for your friendship, our conversations, our laughter and to have each of you in my life.

To Celeste: For answering my questions and providing valuable insights and information. I'm grateful for our conversations and friendship.

To the teachers and administrators who supported Positively Influencing Everyone (PIE) Club and the Food Giveaways: Michelle, Brandi, Brenda, Mark, Sarah, Melissa, Amy, Ray, Lee Ann, and so many more. Thank you for sponsoring the club and taking on added responsibility to support the teens. It is an honor to know you.

To the board and volunteers of Positively Impacting Communities: Andrea, Diana, Wanda, Ginger, Nancy, Liza, Carrie, John, Nancy, Anne, Crystal, Johnna, Cheryl, Lorena, Dawn, Sheri, Leti, Guy, Kat, Carol, Sam, Sandee, Matt, Kim, and all our Prayer Partners: thank you for being part of the ministry, pouring your hearts and time into the youth and families we supported. I'm grateful for the privilege of serving with you.

And to everyone who reached out to me on Facebook with encouraging words, support, and interest as I shared part of my past and the journey of writing this book: Your comments, likes, loves, and cares mean more than you know.

You all mean so much to me. I love you.

Thank you to my editing team: Elizabeth for asking the questions that helped me dig deeper to supply the needed details; Courtney for copyediting and providing valuable information; Beth for your guidance, keen eye for detail, and proficiency with the written word; Karen for your knowledge and thoroughness so the references were cited professionally and correctly; and Christina for your expertise, proofreading with impeccable detail and ensuring the final version was ready for printing. Thank you all for helping me fine-tune my story and information so it can help others.

And thank you to Sarah for creating an engaging cover that portrays the story, detail with the interior design, and walking me through aspects of the printing process. I'm so grateful for your creativity and guidance.

About the Author

Photo credit Brenda Marafioto

Dee Dee Said speaks against violence while advocating for healthy relationships. In addition to her full-time work in the nonprofit sector, she volunteered with youth for seven years, mentoring and engaging them to learn about healthy character traits and to be aware of risks associated with what many deem "normal" teenage activity. With the help of others, she also created opportunities for teens to help youth and families in their community.

Dee Dee treasures spending time with her kids, family, and friends. In her free time, she enjoys running along the San Antonio Riverwalk, cycling, and hiking.

Learn more at Building Strong Foundations
BSFtoday.com

Made in United States
North Haven, CT
28 February 2023

33360223R00174